Financial Management

Financial Management

S. Adaikala Charles
Senior Lecturer
Department of Commerce & Business Administration
T. B. M. L. College, Porayar, Nagai District (TN)

SERIALS PUBLICATIONS
NEW DELHI

First Published–2009

ISBN: 978-81-8387-253-9

Published by

SERIALS PUBLICATIONS
4830/24, Prahlad Street, Ansari Road
Darya Ganj, New Delhi-110002 (India)
Phone : 23245225 Fax : 91-11-23272135
E-mail: serials@satyam.net.in

CONTENTS

Preface *vii*

1. Nature and Scope of Financial Management 1
2. Cost of Capital 5
3. Leverages 63
4. Capital Structure 110
5. Capital Budgeting 146
6. Financial Planning and Forecasting 200

PREFACE

I have great pleasure in bringing out my first book titled "Financial Management-Theory Problems and Solutions". Financial Management is generally regarded as a complete subject of a technological nature. This book presents the subject in a simple, systematic and lucid manner. Solved problems of all models, with detailed working notes are presented in a granded manner. I confident that the book will facilitate an easy grasp of the subject both the teachers and students will find it highly useful–

I must thank **Rt. Rev. Dr. T. Arul Doss**, the Bishop ofTranquebar and Secretary of T.B.M.L. College, Porayar. And **Dr. G. Jonas Gunasekaran**, the Principal of T.B.M.L. College, Porayar.

I am thankful to Serials Publications, New Delhi for their valuable support to publishing the book over a longtime. My thanks are due to **Start Systems**, Porayar for their neat execution of this work.

Express our deep sense of gratitude to **Dr. A. Rajan**, Principal, RVS. College, Karaikal, **Mr. D. Joel Edwinraj** and **Mr. W. Raja Solomon**, Department of Co-operation, TBML College, Porayar, Who initiated me in to writng of this book. I extend my heartfelt thanks due to **Mr. G. Anbalagan** and **Mr. A. Rajasekar**, TBML College, Porayar and **Dr. A. Navinkumar**, Reader in Economics, for their valuable help to bring out the book.

Lastly, I thank my dear **Wife, Sister** and **Brother-in-law** for their constant support and encouragement in this regard.

Also, I thank our Colleagues, Professors and Students of various colleges for their overwhelming support to this book.

Your solicit suggestions for the improvement of the book.

S. Adaikala Charles

Chapter 1

NATURE AND SCOPE OF FINANCIAL MANAGEMENT

Meaning

i. Financial Management deals with raising of resources and utilization of such resources.

ii. It is that specified function of general management.

iii. Financial management is that managerial activity concerned with planning and controlling of the financial resources of the firms or company's.

Definition

According to *Earnest Walter*

"Financial Management is application of planning and controlling functions to the financial functions".

According to *A. K. Sah,*

"Financial Management is dynamic process of planning, organizing, coordinating and controlling of finance in relation to organization function effectively to accomplish the objectives of the organization".

Nature of Financial Management

The nature of financial management includes planning, controlling, the long term, short term financial needs of the firm.

Scope of financial management.

1. Traditional Approaches
2. Outsider–looking in approach
3. Ignored routine problems

4. Ignored non corporate enterprises.
5. Ignored working capital financing.
6. No emphasis on allocation of funds.
7. Modern Approach.
8. Funds requirement decisions.
9. Financing decisions.
10. Investment decisions.
11. Dividend decisions.

Role of Finance Manager in the Changing Scenario

1. Financial decisions
2. Investment decisions
3. Dividend decisions

The dividend decision has also to be taken by the finance manager in the overall global scenario, portfolio opportunities in and outside the country and internal financial needs of his business unit.

The following are the positive benefit to the Indian Industry

i. There has been boost in trade and commerce
ii. There has been sizeable increase in the number of foreign collaborations resulting in transfer latest technologies to the country
iii. Optimum utilization of finance material and human resources which has led to the improvement in overall efficiency
iv. Larger capital inflows resulting in greater industrialization besides strengthening the foreign exchange reserve position.
v. Development of infrastructural facilities and new financial instruments.

Methods of Financial Management

1. Measuring the effectiveness of firm's actions and decisions
2. Measuring the validity of the decisions regarding accepting or rejecting future projects.

3. Cost of capital
4. Financial leverage or Trading on equity
5. Capital budgeting Appraisal methods
6. ABC analysis, cash Management models, Aging schedule of inventories, debtors, turn over ratio, etc.,
7. Ratio Analysis
8. Funds flow analysis and cash flow analysis

Objectives of Financial Management

Financial Management of firm has three important objectives they are

i. investment decisions
ii. Financing decisions
iii. Dividend decisions

There are two types of goals in financial management of any organization.

i. Goal of profit maximization
ii. Goal of wealth maximization

i. Goal of profit maximization

1. Each and every company collect its finance by way of issue of shares.
2. Main objectives is to earn maximum profit of the firm
3. Taking care of all mechanical requirements
4. Record keeping and reporting.
5. Cash planning and credit planning management.

ii. Goal of wealth maximization

1. It is known as value maximization or Net present worth maximization
2. It is based on the concept of cash inflow and outflow
3. Maximizing the Net present value or wealth in the course of business operation.

Importance of Financial Management

1. Successful promotion depends on financial administration.
2. Smooth running and business enterprise
3. Co-ordination of various functional department activities
4. Focal point of decision making
5. Determination of business success
6. Measure of performance

Relationship between Financial Management and other Areas of Management

1. Financial Management and cost accounting
2. Financial Management and Marketing
3. Financial Management and assets Management
4. Financial Management and personnel Management
5. Financial Management and Financial Accounting
6. Financial Management and Strategic Management.

Chapter 2

COST OF CAPITAL

Determination or Computation of Cost of Capital

Meaning

It is minimum required rate of earnings or cut off rate of capital expenditure.

Definition

According to Solomon Ezra, "cost of capital is the minimum required rate of earning or cut off rate of capital expenditure".

Hampton John–defines cost of capital "as the rate of return the firm requires from investments in order to increase the value of the firm in the market place".

Significance of the Cost of Capital

Cost of capital can also be used as a basis for evaluating the performance of a firm and it further helps management in taking so many other financial decisions.

1. As an acceptant criterion in capital budgeting
2. As a determinant of capital mix in capital structure decisions.
3. As a basis for evaluating the financial performance
4. As a basis for making other financial decisions.

Importance of Cost of Capital

1. Capital budgeting decisions
2. Capital structure decisions

Classification of Cost of Capital

1. Explicit cost and implicit cost
2. Future cost and historical cost
3. Specific cost and combined cost
4. Average cost and marginal cost

Controversy Regarding Cost of Capital

1. Traditional approach
2. Modigliani and Miller approach
   1. *Traditional Approach:* According to this approach a firm's cost of capital depends upon the method and level of financing or its capital structure. A firm can therefore, change its overall cost of capital by increasing or decreasing the debt-equity mix.

      But the raising of funds through debenture is cheaper because of the following reasons.
      - i. Interest rates are usually lower than dividend rates.
      - ii. Interest is allowed as an expense resulting while computing taxable profits of the company.
   2. *Modigliani and Miller Approach:* According to this approach the corporations total cost of capital is constant and it is independent of the method and level of financing.

Assumptions Under Modigliani–Miller Approach

The modigliani–Miller approach is subject to the following assumptions.

i. Perfect capital Market

   The securities are traded in perfect capital markets.

   This implies that.

   (a) The investors are free to buy or sell securities.

   (b) The investors are completely knowledgeble and rational persons.

   (c) The purchase and sale of securities involve no cost such as broker's commission, transfer, fees etc.

(d) The investors can borrow against Securities without restriction on the same terms and conditions as the firm can.

ii. Firms can be grouped in homogeneous classes

iii. Same expectation

iv. No corporate taxes

Determination of Cost of Capital Problems in Determination

1. Controversy regarding the dependence of cost of capital upon the method and level of financing.
2. Computation of cost of equity.
3. Computation of cost of retained earnings and depreciation funds.
4. Future costs versus historical costs.
5. Problem of weights.

Computation of Cost of Capital

Computation of cost of capital involves.

i. Computation of cost of each specific source of finance-termed as computation of specific cost.

ii. Computation of composite cost termed as weighted average cost.

Computation of Specific Cost

Cost of each specific source of fiancé, viz. debt, preference capital and equity capital can be determined as follows.

1. Cost of Debt

Debt may be issued at par, at premium or discount. It may be perpectual or redeemable.

(a) When debt is issued at par:

$$kd = [1 - T]\, R$$

where kd = cost of debt, T = Marginal tax rate

R = Debenture interest rate

(b) When debt is issued at premium or discount

$$kd = \frac{I}{NP}(1-T)$$

where kd = cost of debt

I = Annual Interest Payment

NP = Net proceeds of loans or debentures

T = Tax rate

(c) Cost of redeemable debt:

$$\text{kd (before tax)} = \frac{I+\left[\frac{P-NP}{N}\right]}{\left[\frac{P+NP}{2}\right]}$$

where I = Annual Interest payment

P = Par value of debentures

NP = Net Proceeds of debenture

N = Number of years of maturity.

2. Cost of preference capital

The computation of the cost of preference capital poses some conceptual problems. In case of borrowings. There is a legal obligation on the firm to pay interest at fixed rates while in case of preference shares, there is no such legal obligation.

$$\text{Kp} = \frac{\text{DP}}{\text{NP}}$$

Where KP = cost of preference share capital

DP = Fixed preference dividend

NP = Net proceeds of preference share

3. Cost of redeemable preference shares

In case of redeemable preference shares, the cost of capital is the discount rate that equals the net proceeds of sale of preference shares with the present value of future, dividend and principal repayment.

4. Cost of equity capital

   The computation of the cost of equity capital is a difficult task. Some people argue, as observed in case of preference shares, that the equity capital does not involve any costs.

   The rate of return could be considered as the cost of equity capital. It may be divided into the following categories.

   1. The external equity or new issue of equity shares
   2. The retained earnings.

1. The external equity or new issue of equity shares

   i. Dividends price (D/P) approach

   The discount rate that equates the present value of all expected future dividend per share with the net proceeds of the sale [(or) the current market price] of a share.

$$Ke = \frac{D}{NP}$$

Ke = cost of equity capital

D = Dividend per equity share

NP = Net proceeds of an equity shares

The cost of equity on the basis of market price of the company's shares.

$$Ke = \frac{D}{MP}$$

Where ke = cost of equity capital

D = dividend per equity share

MP = Market price of an equity shares

ii. Dividend price plus growth (D/P + g) approach

$$ke = \frac{D}{NP} + G$$

where ke = cost of equity capital

D = Expected dividend per share

NP = Net proceeds per share

G = Growth in expected dividend

iii. Earning price (E/P) approach

$$ke = \frac{E}{NP}$$

where ke = cost of equity capital

E = Earning per share

NP = Net proceeds of an equity share

iv. Realised yield approach

According to this approach, the cost of equity capital should be determined on the basis of return actually realized by the investors in a company on their equity shares.

2. Cost of retained earnings.

   The companies do not generally distribute the entire profits earned by them by way of dividend among their shareholder.

   i. Income tax adjustment
   ii. Brokerage cost adjustment

Weighted Average Cost of Capital

After calculating the cost of each component of capital, the average cost of capital is generally, calculated on the basis of weighted average method.

1. Calculation of the cost of each specific source of funds
2. Assigning weight to specific costs.
   a. Marginal weights method
   b. Historical weights method
3. Adding of the weighted cost of all sources of funds to get an overall weighted average cost of capital

   Weighted average cost of capital can be computed as follows.

$$KW = \frac{\sum XW}{\sum W}$$

Where KW = Weighted average cost of capital

X = Cost of specific source of finance
W = Weight, proportion of specific source of finance

MARGINAL COST OF CAPITAL

Some times, we may be required to calculate the cost of additional funds to be raised, called the marginal cost of capital. The marginal cost of capital is the weighted average cost of new capital calculated by using the marginal weighted. The marginal weights represent the proportion of various sources of funds to be employed in raising additional funds.

COST OF EQUITY USING CAPITAL ASSETS RAISING MODEL (CPAM)

The value of an equity share is a function of cash inflows expected by the investors and the risk associated with the cash inflows. It is calculated by discounting the future scheme of dividend at the required rate of return depends upon the element of risk associated with investment in the share of the business, it will not be difficult to ascertain the total funds required for the purchase of fixed assets.

FACTORS DETERMINING FIXED CAPITAL

The amount of fixed capital requirements of a business depends basically on the following factors:

1. Nature of the business
2. Size of the business
3. Types of products
4. Diversity of production lines
5. Methods of production
6. Method of acquisition of fixed assets

MANAGEMENT OF FIXED CAPITAL

Management of fixed capital is concerned with the raising of required fixed capital at minimum cost and its effective utilization. The following principles should be observed in order to have an efficient management of fixed capital.

1. To increase the earning capacity of the business
2. Feasible fixed assets, hire purchase system
3. Available at lower prices
4. Any idle capacity
5. Maintenance properly, periodical inspection, over haul and scheduled repairs
6. Proper depreciation
7. Investment in fixed assets
8. Requirements of fixed capital

Working Capital Requirement

The term working capital refers to the capital required for day to day operations of a business enterprise. It is represented by excess of current assets over current liabilities. It is necessary for any organization to run successfully its affairs to provide for adequate working capital.

Factors Determining Working Capital

1. Production policies
2. Nature of the business
3. Length of the manufacturing process
4. Credit policy
5. Rapidity of turn over
6. Seasonal fluctuations
7. Fluctuation of supply

Estimation of the Amount of Different Components of Working Capital

The procedure for estimating the amount of each of the constituents of working capital and the information required for the purpose are discussed below.

1. Inventories

   The term "inventories" includes stock of raw material work-in-progress and finished goods. The estimations of each of them will be made as follows.

   a. Stock of raw material
   b. Work in progress
   c. Finished goods
2. Sundry Debtors

   The amount of funds locked up in sundry debtors will be computed on the basis of credit sales and the time–lag in collecting payment.
3. Cash and Bank Balances.

   The amount of money to be kept as cash in hand or cash at bank can be estimated on the basis of past experience.
4. Sundry Creditors.

   The lag in payment to suppliers of raw materials goods etc. and the likely credit purchase to be made during the period will help in estimating the amount of creditors.
5. Outstanding Expenses

   The time–lag in payment of wages and other expenses will help in estimating the amount of outstanding expenses.

PRACTICAL PROBLEMS

1. Cost of Irredeemable Debt
   a. Issued at par
   b. Issued at premium
   c. Issued at Discount

a. Issued at par

Jude Industrial Ltd issues 5,000 12% debentures of Rs.100 each at par. The tax rate is 40% calculate before tax and after tax cost of debt.

Solution :

$$\text{Before tax cost of debt (kd)} = \frac{\text{Interest}}{\text{Net Proceeds}} \times 100$$

$$\text{After tax cost of debt (kd)} = \frac{\text{Interest-Tax}}{\text{Net Proceeds}} \times 100$$

Interest (5,000 x 100 = 5,00,000 x 12%) = 60,000

Less: Tax (60,000x40%) = 24,000

Interest–Tax = 36,000

Net Proceeds (5000x100) = 5,00,000

$$\text{Before tax cost of debt (kd)} = \frac{60{,}000}{5{,}00{,}000} \times 100 = 12\%$$

$$\text{After tax cost of debt (kd)} = \frac{36{,}000}{5{,}00{,}000} \times 100 = 7.2\%$$

2. A Company issued 10% irredeemable of Rs.1,00,000. The company is 55% tax rate. Calculate cost of debt before and after tax.

Solution :

$$\text{Before tax cost of debt (kd)} = \frac{\text{Interest}}{\text{Net Proceeds}} \times 100$$

$$\text{After tax cost of debt (kd)} = \frac{\text{Interest-Tax}}{\text{Net Proceeds}} \times 100$$

Interest (1,00,000 x 10%) = 10,000

Less: Tax (10,000 x 55%) = 5,500

Interest–Tax = 4,500

Net proceeds = 1,00,000

$$\text{Before tax cost of debt (kd)} = \frac{10{,}000}{1{,}00{,}000} \times 100 = 10\%$$

$$\text{After tax cost of debt (kd)} = \frac{4{,}500}{1{,}00{,}000} \times 100 = 4.5\%$$

b. *Issued at a premium*

3. Victory Ltd issued Rs.2,00,000 9% debentures of a premium of 10%. The floatation (issue expenses) were 2%. The tax rate is 40% compute the cost of debt before tax and after tax.

Solution :

$$\text{Before tax cost of debt (kd)} = \frac{\text{Interest}}{\text{Net Proceeds}} \times 100$$

$$\text{After tax cost of debt (kd)} = \frac{\text{Interest-Tax}}{\text{Net Proceeds}} \times 100$$

Interest (2,00,000 × 9%) = 18,000
Less: Tax (18,000 × 40%) = 7,200
Interest – Tax = 10,800
Net Proceeds:
Face value of debentures = 2,00,000
Add: Premium (2,00,000 × 10%) = 20,000
Issue price = 2,20,000
Less: Floatation costs (2,00,000 × 2%) = 4000
Net proceeds = 2,16,000

$$\text{Before tax cost of debt (kd)} = \frac{18,000}{2,16,000} \times 100 = 8.33\%$$

$$\text{After tax cost of debt (kd)} = \frac{10,800}{2,16,00} \times 100 = 5\%$$

4. X company issue 50,000 8% debentures of the face value Re.1 at a premium of 10% cost of issue is 2% Income tax rate is 60% calculate the cost of debt before tax and after tax.

Solution :

$$\text{Before tax cost of debt (kd)} = \frac{\text{Interest}}{\text{Net Proceeds}} \times 100$$

$$\text{After tax cost of debt (kd)} = \frac{\text{Interest-Tax}}{\text{Net Proceeds}} \times 100$$

Interest (50,000 × 1 = 50,000 × 8%) = 4,000
Less: Tax (4,000 × 60%) = 2,400
Interest – Tax = 1,600

Net Proceeds:

Face value of debentures	=	50,000
Add: Premium (50,000x10%)	=	5,000
Issue price	=	55,000
Less: costs (50,000x2%)	=	1,000
Net proceeds	=	54,000

Before tax cost of debt (kd) $= \frac{4,000}{54,000} \times 100 = 7.4\%$

After tax cost of debt (kd) $= \frac{1,600}{54,000} \times 100 = 2.96\%$

c. *Issued at a discount*

5. Jaya ltd issued Rs.60,000 10% debentures of a. discount of 5%. The issue expenses were Rs.2,000 Assuming a tax rate of 40% compute the before tax and after tax cost of debt.

Solution :

Before tax cost of debt (kd) $= \frac{\text{Interest}}{\text{Net Proceeds}} \times 100$

After tax cost of debt (kd) $= \frac{\text{Interest-Tax}}{\text{Net Proceeds}} \times 100$

Interest (60,000 x 10%)	=	6,000
Less: Tax (6,000 x 40%)	=	2,400
Interest – Tax	=	3,600

Net Proceeds:

Face value of debentures	=	60,000
Less: Discount (60,000 × 5%)	=	3,000
Issue price	=	57,000
Less: Issue expenses	=	2,000
Net proceeds	=	55,000

Before tax cost of debt (kd) $= \frac{6,000}{55,000} \times 100 = 10.91\%$

$$\text{After tax cost of debt (kd)} = \frac{3{,}600}{55{,}000} \times 100 = 6.55\%$$

6. A company issue 10,000 10% debentures of the face value of Rs. 10 each at a discount of 10% cost of issue is 3%. Income tax rate is 80%. Calculate the cost of debt before tax and after tax.

Solution :

$$\text{Before tax cost of debt (kd)} = \frac{\text{Interest}}{\text{Net Proceeds}} \times 100$$

$$\text{After tax cost of debt (kd)} = \frac{\text{Interest-Tax}}{\text{Net Proceeds}} \times 100$$

Interest (10,000 × 10 = 1,00,000 × 10%) = 10,000
Less: Tax (10,000 × 80%) = 8,000
Interest – Tax = 2,000
Net Proceeds:
Face value of debentures = 1,00,000
Less: Discount (1,00,000 × 10%) = 10,000
Issue price = 90,000
Less: Expenses (1,00,000 × 3%) = 3000
Net proceeds = 87,000

$$\text{Before tax cost of debt (kd)} = \frac{10{,}000}{87{,}000} \times 100 = 11.49\%$$

$$\text{After tax cost of debt (kd)} = \frac{2{,}00}{87{,}000} \times 100 = 2.29\%$$

7. Tamilvanan Industries ltd issued 10,000 10% debentures of Rs.100 each. The tax rate is 50%. Calculate the before tax and after tax cost of debt if the debentures are issued.

   (a) at par, (b) at premium of 10% (c) at a discount of 10%.

Solution :

$$\text{Before tax cost of debt (kd)} = \frac{\text{Interest}}{\text{Net Proceeds}} \times 100$$

$$\text{After tax cost of debt (kd)} = \frac{\text{Interest-Tax}}{\text{Net Proceeds}} \times 100$$

Interest (10,000 × 100 = 10,00,000 × 10%) = 1,00,000

Less: Tax (1,00,000 × 50%) = 50,000

Interest – Tax = 50,000

Face value of debentures (10,000 × 100) = 10,00,000

a. *Debentures issued at par*

Net proceeds = 10,00,000

$$\text{Before tax cost of debt (kd)} = \frac{1,00,000}{10,00,000} \times 100 = 10\%$$

$$\text{After tax cost of debt (kd)} = \frac{50,000}{10,00,000} \times 100 = 5\%$$

b. *Debentures issued at a premium of 10%*

Net proceeds (10,00,000 + 10% premium)

$$10,00,000 + (10,00,000 \times \frac{10}{100})$$

10,00,000 + 1,00,000 = 11,00,000

$$\text{Before tax cost of debt (kd)} = \frac{1,00,000}{11,00,000} \times 100 = 9\%$$

$$\text{After tax cost of debt (kd)} = \frac{50,800}{11,00,000} \times 100 = 4.55\%$$

c. *Debentures issued at a Discount of 10%*

Net proceeds (10,00,000 – 10% Discount)

$$10,00,000 - (10,00,000 \times \frac{10}{100})$$

10,00,000 - 1,00,000 = 9,00,000

Before tax cost of debt (kd) $= \dfrac{1,00,000}{9,00,000} \times 100 = 11.11\%$

After tax cost of debt (kd) $= \dfrac{50,000}{9,00,000} \times 100 = 5.55\%$

8. Vinoth ltd issued Rs. 5,00,000 8% debt of Rs. 10 each. The rate tax applicable to the company 60% compute the cost of debt when it is issued.

   (a) at par, (b) at Premium 10%, (c) at discount 10%

Solution :

Before tax cost of debt (kd) $= \dfrac{\text{Interest}}{\text{Net Proceeds}} \times 100$

After tax cost of debt (kd) $= \dfrac{\text{Interest-Tax}}{\text{Net Proceeds}} \times 100$

Interest (5,00,000 × 8%) = 40,000

Less: Tax (40,000 × 60%) = 24,000

Interest–Tax = 16,000

Face value of debentures = 5,00,000

a. *Debentures issued at par*

Net proceeds = 5,00,000

Before tax cost of debt (kd) $= \dfrac{40,000}{5,00,000} \times 100 = 8\%$

After tax cost of debt (kd) $= \dfrac{16,000}{5,00,000} \times 100 = 3.2\%$

b. *Debentures issued at a premium of 10%*

Net proceeds = (5,00,000 + 10% premium)

5,00,000 + (5,00,000 × 10%)

5,00,000 + 50,000 = 5,50,000

Before tax cost of debt (kd) $= \dfrac{40,000}{5,50,000} \times 100 = 7.27\%$

After tax cost of debt (kd) $= \frac{16,000}{5,50,000} \times 100 = 2.91\%$

c. *Debentures issued at a discount of 10%*

Net proceeds = (5,00,000 - Discount 10%)

5,00,000 - (5,00,000 × 10%)

5,00,000 - 50,000 = 4,50,000

Before tax cost of debt (kd) $= \frac{40,000}{4,50,000} \times 100 = 8.88\%$

After tax cost of debt (kd) $= \frac{16,000}{4,50,000} \times 100 = 3.55\%$

9. Lilly ltd issued Rs. 10,00,000 8% debt of Rs. 10 each. The tax applicable to the company 60% cost of issue is 4% compute the cost of debt. When it is issued at par at premium 5% and at discount 10%.

Solution :

Before tax cost of debt (kd) $= \frac{\text{Interest}}{\text{Net Proceeds}} \times 100$

After tax cost of debt (kd) $= \frac{\text{Interest-Tax}}{\text{Net Proceeds}} \times 100$

Interest (10,00,000 × 8%)	=	80,000
Less: Tax (80,000 × 60%)	=	48,000
Interest – Tax	=	32,000

a. *Debentures issued at par*

Net proceeds = 10,00,000 – [10, 00,000×4%] = 9,60,000

Before tax cost of debt (kd) $= \frac{80,000}{9,60,000} \times 100 = 8\%$

After tax cost of debt (kd) $= \frac{32,000}{9,60,000} \times 100 = 3.2\%$

b. *Debentures issued at a premium of 5%*

Net proceeds = (10,00,000 + premium 5%)- Expenses

10,00,000 + (10,00,000 × 5%) – (10,00,000 x 4%)

10,00,000 + 50,000 – 40,000 = 10,10,000

$$\text{Before tax cost of debt (kd)} = \frac{80,000}{10,10,000} \times 100 = 7.92\%$$

$$\text{After tax cost of debt (kd)} = \frac{32,000}{10,10,000} \times 100 = 3.62\%$$

c. *Debentures issued at a discount of 10%*

Net proceeds = (10,00,000 - (10% discount) - Expenses

10,00,000 – (10,00,000 × 10%) – (10,00,000 x 4%)

10,00,000 – 1,00,000 – 40,000 = 8,60,000

$$\text{Before tax cost of debt (kd)} = \frac{80,000}{8,60,000} \times 100 = 9.30\%$$

$$\text{After tax cost of debt (kd)} = \frac{32,000}{8,60,000} \times 100 = 3.72\%$$

2. Redeemable Debt
   a. Issued at par
   b. Issued at premium
   c. Issued at discount

a. *Issued at Par*

10. A firm issue debentures of Rs. 1,00,000 and realizes Rs. 98,000 after allowing 2% commission to brokers. The debentures carry an interest rate of 10%. The debentures are due for maturity at the end of the 10th year.

    Calculate of the effective cost of debt before tax.

Solution :

$$\text{Before tax cost of debt (kd)} = \frac{\text{Annual cos before tax}}{\text{Average value of debt}} \times 100$$

Annual cost before tax

Interest (1,00,000 x 10%) = 10,000

Add: Commission (1,00,000 x 2%) = 2,000/10 years = 200

Annual cost before tax = 10,200

Average value of debt.

Issue price = 1,00,000

Less: commission (1,00,000 x 2%) = 2,000

Net proceeds (NP) = 98,000

Redemption Value (RV) = 1,00,000

$$\text{Average value} = \frac{\text{NP+RV}}{2} = \frac{98,000 + 1,00,000}{2} = 99,000$$

$$\text{Before tax cost of debt (kd)} \ \frac{10,200}{99,000} \times 100 = 10.30\%$$

Note: The debentures are redeemable after 10 years. Hence commission is spread over 10 years

b. *Issued at a premium*

11. Venus ltd. Issued 10,000 9% debentures of Rs. 100 each at a premium of 5%. The maturity period is 5 years and the tax rate is 50% compute the cost of debentures to the company if the debentures are redeemable at par.

Solution :

$$\text{Before tax cost of debt (kd)} = \frac{\text{Annual cost before tax}}{\text{Average value of debt}} \times 100$$

After tax cost of debentures (kd)

$$= \frac{\text{Annual cost after tax}}{\text{Average value of debt}} \times 100$$

Annual cost before tax

Interest (10,000 × 100 = 10,00,000 × 9%) = 90,000

Less: Premium (10,00,000 × 5%) = 50,000 ÷ 5 years = 10,000

Annual cost before tax = 80,000

Less: Tax (80,000x50%) = 40,000

Annual cost after tax = 40,000

Average value of debt.

Net proceeds (NP) = (10,00,000 + Premium) = 10,50,000

10,00,000 + (10,00,000 × 5%)

10,00,000 + 50,000

Redemption value (RV) = 10,00,000

$$\text{Average value} = \frac{NP+RV}{2} = \frac{10{,}50{,}000+10{,}00{,}000}{2} = 10{,}25{,}000$$

$$\text{Before tax cost of debt (kd)} = \frac{80{,}000}{10{,}25{,}000}\times 100 = 7.80\%$$

$$\text{After tax cost of debt (kd)} = \frac{40{,}000}{10{,}25{,}000}\times 100 = 3.90\%$$

c. *Issued at a discount*

12. Sunrise ltd issues Rs. 50,000 12% redeemable debentures at a discount of 10%. The floatation costs are 4% and the debentures are redeemable after 5 years. Calculate before tax and after tax cost of debt assuming a tax rate of 40%.

Solution :

Before tax cost of debt (kd)

$$= \frac{\text{Annual cost before tax}}{\text{Average value of debt}}\times 100$$

After tax cost of debentures (kd)

$$= \frac{\text{Annual cost after tax}}{\text{Average value of debt}}\times 100$$

Annual cost before tax

Interest (50,00,000 × 12%) = 6,00,000

Add: Discount (50,00,000 × 10% = 5,00,000 ÷ 5 yrs)

= 1,00,000

Add: Floatation cost (50,00,000 × 4% = 2,00,000 ÷ 5)

= 40,000

Before tax cost = 7,40,000

Less: Tax (7,40,000 × 40%) = 2,96,000

After tax cost = 4,44,000

Average value of debt

Face value of debentures = 50,00,000

Less: Discount (50,00,000 × 10%)

= 5,00,000

Issue Price = 45,00,000

Less: floatation costs (50,00,000 × 4%)

= 2,00,000

Net proceeds (NP) = 43,00,000

Redemption value (RV) = 50,00,000

$$\text{Average value} = \frac{NP + RV}{2} = \frac{43{,}00{,}000 + 50{,}00{,}000}{2}$$

$$= 46{,}50{,}000$$

$$\text{Before tax cost of debt (kd)} = \frac{7{,}40{,}000}{46{,}50{,}000} \times 100 = 15.91\%$$

$$\text{After tax cost of debt (kd)} = \frac{4{,}44{,}000}{46{,}50{,}000} \times 100 = 9.55\%$$

13. A company issued 5,000 12% debentures of Rs.100 each at a discount of 5%. Commission on payable is Rs.25,000. Debentures are repayable after 5 years. Calculate the cost of debentures after tax assuming tax 50%.

Solution :

$$\text{Before tax cost of debt (kd)} = \frac{\text{Annual cost before tax}}{\text{Average value of debt}} \times 100$$

After tax cost of debentures (kd)

$$= \frac{\text{Annual cost after tax}}{\text{Average value of debt}} \times 100$$

Annual cost before tax

Interest (5,000 × 100 = 5,00,000 × 12%) = 60,000

Add: Discount (5,00,000x5% = 25,000 ÷ 5 yrs) = 5,000

= 65,000

Add: Commission (25,000 ÷ 5 years) = 5,000

Before tax cost = 70,000

Less: Tax (70,000 × 50%) = 35,000

After tax cost = 35,000

Average value of debt

Face value of debentures = 5,00,000

Less: Discount (5,00,000 × 5%) = 25,000

Issue Price = 4,75,000

Less: Commission = 25,000

Net proceeds (NP) = 4,50,000

Redemption value (RV) = 5,00,000

$$\text{Average value} = \frac{NP + RV}{2} = \frac{4,50,000 + 5,00,000}{2}$$

$$= 4,75,000$$

$$\text{Before tax cost of debt (kd)} = \frac{70,000}{4,75,000} \times 100 = 14.74\%$$

$$\text{After tax cost of debt (kd)} = \frac{35,000}{4,75,000} \times 100 = 7.37\%$$

14. A company has 15% perpetual debt of Rs.1,00,000. The tax rate is 35% Determine the cost of capital (before tax as well as after tax) Assuming the debt is issued (a) at par, (b) at 10% discount, (c) at 10% premium. Maturity of the year is 10.

Solution :

$$\text{Before tax cost of debt (kd)} = \frac{\text{Annual cost before tax}}{\text{Average value of debt}} \times 100$$

After tax cost of debentures (kd)

$$= \frac{\text{Annual cost after tax}}{\text{Average value of debt}} \times 100$$

a. *Debt issued at par*

Annual cost before tax

Interest (1,00,000 × 15%) = 15,000

Less: Tax (15,000 × 35%) = 5,250

Annual cost after tax = 9,750

Average value of debt

Net proceeds (NP) = 1,00,000

Redemption value (RV) = 1,00,000

$$\text{Average value} = \frac{NP + RV}{2} = \frac{1,00,000 + 1,00,000}{2} = 1,00,000$$

$$\text{Before tax cost of debt (kd)} = \frac{15,000}{1,00,000} \times 100 = 15\%$$

$$\text{After tax cost of debt (kd)} \frac{9,750}{1,00,000} \times 100 = 9.75\%$$

b. *Debt issued at a 10% discount*

Annual cost before tax

Interest (1,00,000 × 15%) = 15,000

Add: Discount (1,00,000 × 10% = 10,000 ÷ 10 years = 1,000

Before tax cost = 16,000

Less: Income tax (16,000x35%) = 5,600

After tax cost = 10,400

15. A company issues 10% debentures at par for a total value of Rs.10,00,000. The debentures are redeemable after 10 years at a premium 10%. It the tax rate is 40%. Compute the cost of debentures of the company (a) before tax and (b) after tax.

Solution :

$$\text{Before tax cost of debt (kd)} = \frac{\text{Annual cost before tax}}{\text{Average value of debt}} \times 100$$

After tax cost of debentures (kd)

$$= \frac{\text{Annual cost after tax}}{\text{Average value of debt}} \times 100$$

Annual cost before tax

Interest (10,00,000 × 10%) = 1,00,000

Less: Premium 10,00,000 × 10% = 1,00,000 ÷ 10 years
= 10,000

Annual cost before tax = 90,000

Less: Tax (90,000 × 40%) = 36,000

Annual cost after tax = 54,000

Average value of Debt

Net proceeds (NP) = 11,00,000

10,00,000 + Premium 10%

10,00,000 + (10,00,000 × 10%)

10,00,000 + 1,00,000

Redemption value (RV) = 10,00,000

$$\text{Average value} = \frac{NP + RV}{2} = \frac{11,00,000 + 10,00,000}{2}$$

= 10,50,000

$$\text{Before tax cost of debt (kd)} = \frac{90,000}{10,50,000} \times 100 = 8.57\%$$

$$\text{After tax cost of debt (kd)} = \frac{54,000}{10,50,000} \times 100 = 5.14\%$$

16. A company issues 10,000 bonds of Rs. 100 each at 14% p.a. marketing costs are Rs. 20,000. The bonds are to be redeemed after 10 years and the company is taxed at the rate of 40% compute the cost of debt if the bonds are issued.

(a) at par, (b) at a discount of 5% (c) at a premium of 5%

Solution :

$$\text{Before tax cost of debt (kd)} = \frac{\text{Annual cost before tax}}{\text{Average value of debt}} \times 100$$

After tax cost of debentures (kd)

$$= \frac{\text{Annual cost after tax}}{\text{Average value of debt}} \times 100$$

a. *Bonds issued at par*

Interest (10,00,000 × 14%) = 1,40,000

Add: Marketing costs (20,000 ÷ 10 years) = 2,000

Annual cost before tax = 1,42,000

Less: Tax (1,42,000 × 40%) = 56,800

Annual cost after tax = 85,200

Average value of debt

Face value of bonds (100 × 10,000) = 10,00,000

Less : Marketing cost = 20,000

Net proceeds (NP) = 9,80,000

Redemption value (RV) = 10,00,000

$$\text{Average value} = \frac{NP + RV}{2} = \frac{9{,}80{,}000 + 10{,}00{,}000}{2} = 9{,}90{,}000$$

$$\text{Before tax cost of debt (kd)} = \frac{1{,}42{,}000}{9{,}90{,}000} \times 100 = 14.4\%$$

$$\text{After tax cost of debt (kd)} = \frac{85{,}200}{9{,}90{,}000} \times 100 = 8.6\%$$

b. *Bonds issued at a discount of 5%*

Annual cost before tax

Interest (10,00,000 × 14%) = 1,40,000

Add: Marketing costs (20,000 ÷ 10 yrs) = 2,000

= 1,42,000

Add: Discount (10,00,000 × 5% = 50,000 ÷ 10) = 5,000
Annual cost before tax = 1,47,000
Less: Tax (1,47,000 × 40%) = 58,800
Annual cost after tax = 88,200

Average value of debt:
Face value (100 × 10,000) = 10,00,000
Less: Marketing costs 20,000
Discount (10,00,000 × 5%) = 50,000 = 70,000
Net proceeds (NP) = 9,30,000
Redemption value (RV) = 10,00,000

$$\text{Average value} = \frac{NP + RV}{2} = \frac{9,30,000 + 10,00,000}{2}$$

= 9,65,000

$$\text{Before tax cost of debt (kd)} = \frac{1,47,000}{9,65,000} \times 100 = 15.2\%$$

$$\text{After tax cost of debt (kd)} = \frac{88,200}{9,65,000} \times 100 = 9.1\%$$

c. *Bonds issued at a premium of 5%*
Annual cost before tax
Interest (10,00,000 × 14%) = 1,40,000
Add: Marketing cost (20,000 ÷ 10 yrs) = 2,000
= 1,42,000
Less: Premium (10,00,000 × 5% = 50,000 ÷ 10) = 5,000
Annual cost before tax = 1,37,000
Less: Tax (1,37,000 × 40%) = 54,800
Annual cost after tax = 82,200

Average value of debt
Face value of bonds (100 × 10,000) = 10,00,000
Add: Premium (10,00,000 × 5%) = 50,000
= 10,50,000
Less: Marketing costs = 20,000

Net proceeds (NP) = 10,30,000

Redemption value (RV) = 10,00,000

$$\text{Average value} = \frac{NP + RV}{2} = \frac{10,30,000 + 10,00,000}{2}$$

$$= 10,15,000$$

$$\text{Before tax cost of debt (kd)} = \frac{1,37,000}{10,15,000} \times 100 = 13.49\%$$

$$\text{After tax cost of debt (kd)} = \frac{82,200}{10,15,000} \times 100 = 8.09\%$$

17. A Rs.100 par value bond bearing a coupon rate of 12% will mature after 5 years. What is the value of the bond, if the discount rate is 15%?

Solution :

$$\text{Before tax cost of debt (kd)} = \frac{\text{Annual cost before tax}}{\text{Average value of debt}} \times 100$$

After tax cost of debentures (kd)

$$= \frac{\text{Annual cost after tax}}{\text{Average value of debt}} \times 100$$

Bonds issued at a discount of 15%

Interest (100 × 12%) = 12.00

Add: Discount (100 × 15% = 15 ÷ 5 yrs) = 0.75

Annual cost before tax = 12.75

Average value of debt

Face value = 100

Less: Discount (100 × 15%) = 15

Net proceeds (NP) = 85

Redemption value (RV) = 100

$$\text{Average value} = \frac{NP + RV}{2} = \frac{82 + 100}{2} = 92.50$$

$$\text{Before tax cost of debt (kd)} = \frac{12.75}{92.50} \times 100 = 13.78\%$$

18. Consider a bond, maturing in 10 years and having a compound rate of 8%. The par value is Rs. 1000. Investors consider 10% to be an appropriate required rate of return in view of the risk level associated with this bond. Value of the bond.

Bonds issued at par

$$\text{Before tax cost of debt (kd)} = \frac{\text{Annual cost before tax}}{\text{Average value of debt}} \times 100$$

After tax cost of debentures (kd)

$$= \frac{\text{Annual cost after tax}}{\text{Average value of debt}} \times 100$$

Annual cost before tax

Interest (1,000 × 8%) = 80

Add: Expenses (1000 × 10% = 100 ÷ 10yrs) = 10

Annual cost before tax = 90

Average value of debt

Face value = 1000

Less: Expenses (1000 × 10%) = 100

New proceeds (NP) = 900

Redemption value (RV) = 1000

$$\text{Average value} = \frac{NP + RV}{2} = \frac{900 + 1000}{2} = 950$$

$$\text{Cost of debt before tax (kd)} = \frac{90}{950} \times 100 = 9.47\%$$

Preference Share Capital

I. Cost of irredeemable preference share capital

II. Cost of redeemable preference share capital

I. Cost of irredeemable pref. Share capital
   (a) At par
   (b) At premium
   (c) At Discount

19. A company issued 20,000 10% shares of Rs.100 each. The issue expenses were Rs. 2 per share. Calculate the cost of preference share capital if the shares are issued (a) at par, (b) at a premium of 10% (c) at a discount of 5%.

Solution :

$$\text{Cost of Irredeemable P.S. capital} = \frac{\text{Annual Dividend}}{\text{Net Proceeds}} \times 100$$

Annual Dividend

Face value pref. Share capital (100 × 20,000) = 20,00,000

Annual Dividend (20,00,000 × 10%) = 2,00,000

a. *Shares issued at par*

Face value	=	20,00,000
Less: Issue Expenses (20000 × 2)	=	40,000
Net Proceeds (NP)	=	19,60,000

$$\text{Cost of pref. Share capital} = \frac{2,00,000}{19,60,000} \times 100 = 10.2\%$$

b. *Shares issued at a premium of 10%*

Face value	=	20,00,000
Add: Premium (20,00,000 × 10%)	=	2,00,000
	=	22,00,000
Less: Issue Expenses	=	40,000
Net proceeds (NP)	=	21,60,000

$$\text{Cost of pref. Share capital} = \frac{2,00,000}{21,60,000} \times 100 = 9.26\%$$

c. *Shares issued at a discount of 5%*

Face value	=	20,00,000

$$\text{Less: Discount} + [20{,}00{,}000 \times 5\%] = 1{,}00{,}000$$

$$\text{Expenses} \quad [20{,}000 \times 2] \quad = \quad \underline{40{,}000}\ 1{,}40{,}000$$

Net proceeds (NP = 18,60,000

$$\text{Cost of pref. Share capital} = \frac{2{,}00{,}000}{18{,}60{,}000} \times 100 = 10.75\%$$

20. A company raises preferences share capital of Rs.1,00,000 by issues of 10% preference share of Rs.10 each. Calculate the preference share capital when their issued at par, at 10% premium and at 10% discount.

Solution :

$$\text{Cost of Irredeemable P.S. capital} = \frac{\text{Annual Dividend}}{\text{Net Proceeds}} \times 100$$

Face value pref. Share capital = 1,00,000

Annual Dividend (1,00,000 × 10%) = 10,000

a. *Shares issued at par*

Net Proceeds (NP) = 1,00,000

$$\text{Cost of pref. Share capital} = \frac{10{,}000}{1{,}00{,}000} \times 100 = 10\%$$

b. *Shares issued at a premium of 10%*

Face value = 1,00,000

Add: Premium (1,00,000 × 10%) = 10,000

Net proceeds (NP) = 1,10,000

$$\text{Cost of pref. Share capital} = \frac{10{,}000}{1{,}10{,}000} \times 100 = 9.09\%$$

c. *Shares issued at a discount of 10%*

Face value = 1,00,000

Less: Discount (1,00,000 × 10%) = 10,000

Net proceeds (NP) = 90,000

Cost of pref. Share capital = $\frac{10,000}{90,000} \times 100$ = 11.1%

21. A company issues 10,000 10% preference shares of Rs. 100 each at a discount of 5%. The cost of issue is Rs. 2 per share calculate the cost of preference share capital.

Solution :

Shares issued at a discount of 5%

Cost of Irredeemable P.S. capital = $\frac{\text{Annual Dividend}}{\text{Net Proceeds}} \times 100$

Face value of pref. Share capital = 10,000 × 100 = 10,00,000

Annual Dividend (10,00,000 × 10%) = 1,00,000

Face value of pref. Share capital	=	10,00,000
Less: Discount (10,00,000 × 5%)	=	50,000
	=	9,50,000
Less: Issue Expenses (10,000 × 2)	=	20,000
Net Proceeds (NP)	=	9,30,000

Cost of pref. Share capital = $\frac{1,00,000}{9,30,000} \times 100$ = 10.75%

22. A company issues 10,000 10% preference shares of Rs.100 each at a discount of 5%. The cost of issue is Rs.5 per share. Calculate the cost of preference share capital.

Solution :

Cost of Irredeemable P.S. capital = $\frac{\text{Annual Dividend}}{\text{Net Proceeds}} \times 100$

Face value pref. Share capital (10,000 × 100) = 10,00,000

Annual Dividend (10,00,000 × 10%) = 1,00,000

Shares issued at a discount of 5%

Face value of pref. Share capital	=	10,00,000
Less: Discount (10,00,000x5%)	=	50,000
	=	9,50,000
Less: Issue Expenses (10,000 × 5)	=	50,000

Net Proceeds (NP) = 9,00,000

$$\text{Cost of pref. Share capital} = \frac{1,00,000}{9,00,000} \times 100 = 11.1\%$$

23. A company raised preference share capital of Rs.2,00,000 by issues of 10% preference shares of Rs. 10 each. The cost of issues is 2% Brokers commission of 4%. Calculate the cost of preferences share capital when they are issued. (a) at par, (b) at premium 15%, and (c) at discount 20%.

Solution :

$$\text{Cost of Irredeemable P.S. capital} = \frac{\text{Annual Dividend}}{\text{Net Proceeds}} \times 100$$

Face value of pref. Share capital = 2,00,000

Annual Dividend (2,00,000 × 10%) = 20,000

a. *Shares issued at par*

Face value = 2,00,000

Less: Issue Expis (2,00,000 × 2%) 4,000

Commission (2,00,000 × 4%) 8,000 = 12,000

Net Proceeds (NP) = 1,88,000

$$\text{Cost of pref. Share capital} = \frac{20,000}{1,88,000} \times 100 = 10.64\%$$

b. *Share issued at a premium of 15%:–*

Face value = 2,00,000

Add: Premium (2,00,000 × 15%) = 30,000

= 2,30,000

Less: Issue Expenses 4,000

Commission 8,000 = 12,000

Net proceeds (NP) = 2,18,000

$$\text{Cost of pref. Share capital} = \frac{20,000}{2,18,000} \times 100 = 9.17\%$$

c. *Shares issued at a discount of 20%*

Face value = 2,00,000

Less: Discount (2,00,000 × 20%) 40,000

Issue Expenses 4,000

Commission 8,000 = 52,000

Net proceeds (NP) = 1,48,000

$$\text{Cost of pref. Share capital} = \frac{20,000}{1,48,000} \times 100 = 13.51\%$$

II. Cost of Redeemable Pref. Share Capital

24. A company has 10% redeemable preference share, redeemable at the end of the 10th year from the issue the under writing cost came to 2%. calculate the effective cost of preference share capital. When the preference share capital Rs. 1,00,000.

Solution :

Cost of Redeemable pref. Share capital kp

$$= \frac{\text{Annual Dividend}}{\text{Average Value of pref.S.Capital}} \times 100$$

Annual Dividend:

Dividend 1,00,000 × 10% = 10,000

Add: Expenses (1,00,000 × 2%) 2000 ÷ 10 yrs = 200

Annual Dividend = 10,200

Average value

Issue Price = 1,00,000

Less: Expenses (1,00,000 × 2%) = 2,000

Net Proceeds (NP) = 98,000

Redemption value (RV) = 1,00,000

$$\text{Average value} = \frac{NP+RV}{2} = \frac{98,000 + 1,00,000}{2} = 99,000$$

$$\text{Cost of Redeemable pref. Share capital kp} = \frac{10,200}{99,000} \times 100$$

$$= 10.30\%$$

25. A company issued Rs. 1,00,000 15% preference share capital of Rs.100 each redeemable after 7 years. The cost issue of preference share capital came to 3%. Calculate cost of preferences share capital.

Solution :

Cost of Redeemable pref. Share capital (RPS) kp

$$= \frac{\text{Annual Dividend}}{\text{Average Value of pref.S.Capital}} \times 100$$

Annual dividend

Preference Dividend (1,00,000 × 15%)	=	15,000
Add: Expenses (1,00,000 × 3% = 3000 ÷ 7)	=	426
Annual dividend	=	15,429
Average value		
Issue Price	=	1,00,000
Less: Expenses (1,00,000x3%)	=	3,000
Net proceeds (NP)	=	97,000
Redemption value (RV)	=	1,00,000

$$\text{Average value} = \frac{NP+RV}{2} = \frac{97{,}000 + 1{,}00{,}000}{2} = 98{,}500$$

Cost of Redeemable pref. Share capital (RPS) kp

$$= \frac{15{,}429}{98500} \times 100 = 15.67\%$$

26. A company issues 10,000 10% preferences share of rs.100 each redeemable after 10 years at a premium of 5%. The cost of issue is Rs.2 per share. Calculate cost of preference share capital.

Solution :

Cost of Redeemable pref. Share capital (RPS) kp

$$= \frac{\text{Annual Dividend}}{\text{Average Value of pref.S.Capital}} \times 100$$

Annual dividend

Preference Dividend (10,000x100 = 10,00,000 × 10%)

= 1,00,000

Less: Premium (10,00,000 × 5% = 50,000 ÷ 10) = 5,000

= 95,000

Add: Expenses (10,000x2 = 20.000 ÷ 10) = 2,000

Annual dividend = 97,000

Average value

Issue Price (10,000, × 100) = 10,00,000

Less: Expenses (10,000 × 2) = 20,000

Net Proceeds (NP) = 9,80,000

Face Value = 10,00,000

Add: Premium (10,00,000 × 5%). = 50,000

Redemption value (RV) = 10,50,000

$$\text{Average value} = \frac{NP+RV}{2} = \frac{9,80,000+10,50,000}{2}$$

= 10,15,000.

Cost of Redeemable pref. Share capital (RPS) kp

$$= \frac{97,000}{10,15,000} \times 100 = 9.55\%$$

27. A ltd issues 10,000 9% preference share of Rs. 100 each. The shares are redeemable after 10 years at a premium of 5%. Flotation costs are 2%. Calculate the effective cost of redeemable preference share capital.

Solution :

Cost of Redeemable pref. Share capital (RPS) kp

$$= \frac{\text{Annual Dividend}}{\text{Average Value of pref.S.Capital}} \times 100$$

Annual dividend

Preference Dividend (10,000 × 100 = 10,00,000 × 9%) = 90,000

Add: Floatation costs (10,00,000 × 2% = 20.000 ÷ 10) = 2,000

= 92,000

Less: Premium I10,00,000 × 5% = 50,000 ÷ 10) = 5,000

Annual dividend = 87,000

Average value

Issue Price (10,000, × 100) = 10,00,000

Less: Floatation costs (10,00,000 × 2%) = 20,000

= 9,80,000

Add: Premium (10,00,000 × 5%) = 50,000

Net Proceeds (NP) = 10,30,000

Redemption value (RV) = 10,00,000

$$\text{Average value} = \frac{NP+RV}{2} = \frac{10{,}30{,}000+10{,}00{,}000}{2}$$

= 10,15,000.

Cost of Redeemable pref. Share capital (RPS) kp

$$= \frac{87{,}000}{10{,}15{,}000} \times 100 = 8.57\%$$

28. Jayant ltd., issued 5,000 10% preference share of Rs. 100 each at a premium of 10%. The shares are redeemable after 10 years. Floatation costs are 4%. Calculate the effective cost of preference share capital.

Solution :

Cost of Redeemable pref. Share capital (RPS) kp

$$= \frac{\text{Annual Dividend}}{\text{Average Value of pref.S.Capital}} \times 100$$

Annual dividend

Preference Dividend (50,000x100 = 50,00,000x10%)

= 50,000

Add: Floatation costs (5,00,000 × 4% = 20,000 ÷10)

= 2,000

= 52,000

Less: Premium (5,00,000 × 10% = 50.000 ÷ 10) = 5,000

Annual dividend = 47,000

Average value

Face value = 5,00,000

Less: Floatation costs (5,00,000 × 4%) = 20,000

Net Proceeds (NP) = 5,30,000

Redemption value (RV) = 5,00,000

$$\text{Average value} = \frac{NP+RV}{2} = \frac{5,30,000+5,00,000}{2} = 5,15,000.$$

Cost of Redeemable pref. Share capital (RPS) kp

$$= \frac{47,000}{5,15,000} \times 100 = 9.13\%$$

30. B ltd issues 10,000 10% preference shares of Rs. 100 each at a discount of 5%. The shares are redeemable after 10 years and the issue expenses are 4%. Calculate the effective cost of redeemable preference share capital.

Solution :

Cost of Redeemable pref. Share capital (RPS) kp

$$= \frac{\text{Annual Dividend}}{\text{Average Value of pref. S. Capital}} \times 100$$

Annual dividend

Preference Dividend (10,000 × 100 = 10,00,000 × 10%)
= 1,00,000

Add: Expenses (10,00,000 × 4% = 40,000 ÷ 10yrs) = 4,000

Add: Discount (10,00,000 × 5% = 50,000 ÷ 10yrs) = 5,000

Annual dividend = 1,09,000

Average value

Face value (10,000 × 100 = 10,00,000) = 10,00,000

Less: Expenses (10,00,000 × 4%) = 40,000 = 9,60,000

Less: Discount (10,00,000 × 5%) = 50,000

Net Proceeds (NP) = 9,10,000

Redemption value (RV) = 10,00,000

$$\text{Average value} = \frac{NP+RV}{2} = \frac{9,10,000 + 10,00,00}{2} = 9,55,000.$$

Cost of Redeemable pref. Share capital (RPS) kp

$$= \frac{1,09,000}{9,55,000} \times 100 = 11.41\%$$

Cost of Equity Share Capital

I. Dividend yield method or Dividend price method

II. Dividend yield + Growth method

III. Earnings price method

IV. Realized yield method

I. Dividend yield method or dividend price method

31. A company issues one crore equity shares of Rs.100 each at a premium of 10%. The company has been consistently paying a dividend 18% for the past 5 years. It is expected to maintain the dividend in future also.

a. Compute the cost of equity capital

b. What will be the cost of equity capital if the market price of the share is Rs. 200?

Solution :

a. Cost of equity capital (ke) = $\frac{D}{NP} \times 100$

D = Expected dividend per share = 100 × 18% = 18

NP = Net proceeds per share = 100 + premium = 100 + 10 = 110

Cost of equity capital (ke) = $\frac{18}{110} \times 100 = 16.36\%$

b. If the market price is Rs. 200

D = 18

MP= Market price = 200

Cost of equity capital (ke) = $\frac{18}{200} \times 100 = 9\%$

32. Anand Ltd. Offers for public subscription equity shares of Rs.10 each at a premium of 10%. The company pays an underwriting commission of 5% on the issue price. The equity share holders expect a dividend of 15%.
    a. calculate the cost of equity capital
    b. Calculate the cost of equity capital, if the market price of the sahre is Rs. 20.

Solution :

a. Cost of Equity capital

$$\text{cost of equity capital (ke)} = \frac{D}{NP} \times 100$$

$D = 10 \times 15\% = 1.50$

$NP = 10 + (10 \times 10\%) = 10 + 1 \qquad = 11$

Less: underwriting commission (11 × 5%) = 0.55

Net proceeds (NP) = 10.45

$$\text{Cost of equity capital (ke)} = \frac{1.50}{10.45} \times 100 = 14.35\%$$

b. If the market price is Rs. 20:

$$\text{Cost of equity capital (ke)} = \frac{1.50}{20} \times 100 = 7.50\%$$

33. Alpha is a share holder in India polyester ltd. The earnings of the company have varied considerably. Alpha feels that the long run average dividend would be Rs.3 per share. He expects that the same pattern would continue in future. Alpha expects minimum rate of earning of 15%. At what price Alpha should buy the share of the company?

Solution :

$$\text{cost of equity capital (ke)} = \frac{D}{MP} \times 100$$

$$\text{market price} = \frac{3}{0.15} \times 100 = \text{Rs.}20$$

It would be advisable to purchase the share at Rs. 20.

34. The expected average earning per share of a company are Rs.12.50 and the current market price of the share is Rs.90. what is the cost of equity capital.

Solution :

$$\text{Cost of equity capital (ke)} = \frac{D}{MP}\times 100 = \frac{12.50}{90}\times 100$$

$$= 13.89\%$$

35. A company offers for public subscription equity shares of Rs.10 each at a premium of 10%. The company pays 5% of the issue price as underwriting commissions. The rate of dividend expected by the equity share holders is 20%.

You are required to calculate the cost of equity capital. Will your cost of capital be different if it is to be calculated on the present market value of the equity shares which is Rs.15?

Solution :

$$\text{cost of equity capital (ke)} = \frac{D}{MP}\times 100$$

Cost of Equity capital at a premium of 10%

D = 10 × 20%	= 2
Net proceeds	= 10.00
Add: premium (10 × 10%)	= 1.00
	= 11.00
Less: Underwriting commission (10 × 5%)	= 0.50
Market price	= 10.50

$$\text{Cost of equity capital (ke)} = \frac{2}{10.50}\times 100 = 19\%$$

Cost of capital at a premium of 10% and market price is Rs. 15

D = 15 × 20%	= 3
Net proceeds	= 15

Add: Premium (15 × 10%) = $\frac{1.50}{16.50}$

Less: underwriting commission = 0.75

Market price = 15.75

$$\text{Cost of equity capital (ke)} = \frac{3}{15.75} \times 100 = 19\%$$

DIVIDEND YILED + GROWTH METHOD

36. The market price of an equity shares of G LTd is Rs. 80. The dividend expected a year hence is Rs. 1.60 per share. The share holders anticipate a growth of 7% in dividends. Calculate the cost of equity capital.

Solution :

$$\text{Cost of Equity capital (ke)} = \left(\frac{D}{MP} + G\right) \times 100$$

D = Expected Dividend per share = Rs.1.60

MP = Market price per share = Rs.80

G = Growth rate in dividend = 7%

$$\text{Cost of equity capital (ke)} = \left[\frac{1.60}{80} + 0.07\right] \times 100$$

$$= (0.05 + 0.07) \times 100$$

$$= 0.12 \times 100 = 12\%$$

37. The current market price of a company's share is Rs. 100. The company plans to issue new shares to raise Rs. 1,00,00,000. The net proceeds per share will be the market price less the floatation costs which is 5% of the share price.

    If the company plans to pay a dividend of Rs. 4.75 and the growth in dividend is expected to be 8%. Calculate the cost of new issue of equity shares.

Solution :

$$\text{Cost of equity capital (New issue) (ke)} = \left[\frac{D}{NP} + G\right] \times 100$$

D = 4.75,

NP = 100 – Flotation costs = 100 – (100 × 5%) = 100 – 5 = 95

G = 8%

$$\text{Cost of equity capital (ke)} = \left[\frac{4.75}{95} + 0.08\right] \times 100$$

$$= (0.05 + 0.08) \times 100$$

$$= 0.13 \times 100 = 13\%$$

38. A company plans to issue 1,000 shares of Rs.100 each. The floatation cost is 5%. The company pays a dividend of Rs. 10 per share and the growth in dividend is 5%. Compute the cost of new equity share. If the share is currently quoted at market of Rs.150. Calculate the cost of equity.

Solution :

$$\text{Costs of equity capital (New issue)} = \left[\frac{D}{MP} + G\right] \times 100$$

D = 10

NP = 100 – Floatation costs = 100 – 5% = 100 – 5 = 95

$$\text{Costs of Equity capital (old issue)} = \left[\frac{10}{95} + 0.05\right] \times 100$$

$$= (0.11 + 0.05) \times 100 = 0.16 \times 100 = 16\%$$

Cost of Equity capital (New issue)

$$= \left[\frac{D}{MP} + G\right] \times 100$$

$$= \left[\frac{10}{150} + 0.05\right] \times 100$$

$$= (0.07 + 0.05) = 0.12 \times 100 = 12\%$$

39. Your company's share is quoted in the market at Rs. 20 currently. The company pays a dividend of Re 1 per share and the investor's market expects a growth of 5% per year. Compute company's equity share cost of capital.

Solution :

Cost of equity capital (New issue) (ke) = $\left[\frac{D}{NP}+G\right] \times 100$

D = 1, Np = 20, G = 5%

Cost of Equity capital (ke) = $\left[\frac{1}{20}+0.05\right] \times 100$

$= (0.05 + 0.05) \times 100$

$= 0.10 \times 100$

$= 10\%$

40. A company's share is quoted in the market at Rs.40 and the expected dividend for the next year is Rs. 2 per share. Thereafter, the investors expect a growth rate of 5% p.a.
    a. Calculate the cost of equity capital
    b. Calculate the market per share if the expected growth rate is 6% p.a.
    c. Calculate the market price per share if the dividend of Rs. 2 is maintained, the cost of equity is 9% and the expected growth in dividends is 6% p.a.

Solution :

a. cost of equity capital (ke)

$$Ke = \left[\frac{D}{MP}+G\right] \times 100$$

D = 2, MP = 40, G = 5%

$$Ke = \left[\frac{2}{40}+0.05\right] \times 100$$

$$= (0.05 + 0.05) \times 100 = 0.10 \times 100 = 10\%.$$

b. Market price (MP), If growth rate is 6%

$$Ke = \left[\frac{2}{MP} + 6\%\right]$$

$$10\% = \left[\frac{2}{MP} + 6\%\right]$$

$$10\% - 6\% = \left[\frac{2}{MP}\right], 4\% = \left[\frac{2}{MP}\right]$$

$$MP \times 4\% = 2, MP = \left[\frac{2}{4\%}\right] = \left[\frac{2}{0.04}\right] = Rs.50$$

c. Market price (MP), If Growth rate is 6%

$$Ke = \left[\frac{D}{MP} + G\right]$$

$$9\% = \left[\frac{2}{MP} + 6\%\right]$$

$$9\% - 6\% = \left[\frac{2}{MP}\right], 3\% = \left[\frac{2}{MP}\right], MP \times 3\% = 2$$

$$MP = \left[\frac{2}{0.03}\right] = Rs.66.67$$

41. The shares of a company are selling at Rs.50 per share and it had paid a dividend Rs.5 per share last year. The investors expect a growth rate of 5% per year.
   a. Compute the company cost of equity capital.
   b. If the anticipated growth in dividend is 7% p.a., calculate the indicated market price per share.

Solution :

a. Cost of Equity capital (ke)

D = Expected dividend	=	5.00
Add: Growth rate at 5%	=	0.25
	=	5.25

MP = 50, Growth rate = 5.25

$$Ke = \left[\frac{5.25}{50}\right] + 0.05 \times 100 = (0.105 + 0.05) \times 100$$

$$= 0.155 \times 100 = 15.5\%$$

b. Market price (MP), if Growth rate is 7%:

D = Expected dividend = 5.00

Add: Growth rate at 7% = 0.35

= 5.35

$$15.5\% = \left[\frac{5.35}{MP}\right] + 7\%$$

$$15.5\% - 7\% = \left[\frac{5.35}{MP}\right]$$

$$8.5\% \times MP = 5.35$$

$$MP = \left[\frac{5.35}{0.085}\right] = Rs.62.94$$

42. The shares of a steel company are quoted at Rs.42 per share. The firm had paid a dividend of Rs. 4 per share last year. The expected growth in dividend is 5% p.a.
    a. Determine the cost of equity capital of the company.
    b. Determine the market price of the equity share, if the anticipated growth rate of the firm: 1. rises to 8% and 2. falls to 3%.

Solution :

a. cost of equity capital (ke)

$$Ke = \left[\frac{D}{MP} + G\right] \times 100$$

D = Expected dividend = 4.00

Add: Growth rate at 5% = 0.20

= 4.20

MP = 42, G = 5

$$Ke = \left[\frac{4.20}{42} + 0.05\right] \times 100 = (0.10 + 0.05) \times 100$$

$= 0.15 \times 100 = 15\%$

b. Market price, if the Growth rate is 8%

D = Expected dividend = 4.00

Add: Growth rate at 8% = 0.32

= 4.32

$$Ke = \left[\frac{D}{MP} + 8\%\right]$$

$$15\% = \left[\frac{4.32}{MP} + 8\%\right]$$

$$15\% - 8\% = \left[\frac{4.32}{MP}\right],\ 7\% = \left[\frac{4.32}{MP}\right],$$

$$MP \times 7\% = 4.32,$$

$$MP = \left[\frac{4.32}{0.07}\right] = \text{Rs. } 61.71.$$

c. Market price, if the growth rate falls to 3%

D = Expected dividend = 4.00

Add: Growth rate at 3% = 0.12

= 4.12

$$Ke = \left[\frac{D}{MP} + G\right]$$

$$15\% = \left[\frac{4.12}{MP} + 3\%\right]$$

$$15\% - 3\% = \left[\frac{4.12}{MP}\right]$$

$$12\% = \left[\frac{4.12}{MP}\right],\ 12\% \times MP = 4.12$$

$$MP = \left[\frac{4.12}{0.12}\right] = \text{Rs. } 34.33$$

43. A ltd is a mining company. Its iron reserves are being depleted and cost of recovering iron is increasing each year. As a result, the company's earnings and dividends are

declining at the rate of 8% p.a. The previous year's dividend was Rs.10 and the required rate of return is 15%. What would be the market price of the equity share of A Ltd?.

Solution :

$$\text{Cost of Equity capital (ke)} = \left[\frac{D}{MP} + G\right]$$

Ke = cost of equity capital = 15%

D = Expected divided = 10.00

Less: Decline Expected at 8% = 0.80

D = 9.20

$$Ke = \left[\frac{D}{MP} + G\right]$$

$$15\% = \left[\frac{9.20}{MP}\right] - 8\%$$

$$15\% + 8\% = \frac{9.20}{MP},\ MP \times 23\% = 9.20,\ MP = \frac{9.20}{0.23} = \text{Rs. } 40$$

44. The shares of Rose Ltd are currently traded at Rs. 40 per share. The company's dividend record is as follows. 2000-2001 = Rs. 2.20, 2001-2002 = Rs. 2.42, 2002-2003 = Rs. 2.66, 2003-2004 = Rs 2.92, 2004-2005 = Rs.3.22.

    Rose Ltd. plans to issue new equity shares at Rs.40. The floatation costs are estimated at 5% of the issue price. You are required to determine

    a. Growth rate is dividends.
    b. Cost of equity capital assuming that growth in dividends will continue at the same time.
    c. Cost of new equity shares.

Solution :

a. Growth rate in dividends (G)

During the 5 years from 2000-2001 to 2004-2005 dividend had increased from Rs.2.20 to Rs.3.22.

$$\text{The compound factor} = \frac{3.22}{2.20} = 1.464$$

In the compound factor table, the compound factor 1.464 in the row of 4 years is found in the 10% column. Hence, growth rate in dividends is 10%

b. Cost of equity capital (ke)

$$Ke = \left[\frac{D}{MP} + G\right] \times 100$$

D = Expected dividend = 3.22

Add: Growth (3.22x10%) = 0.32

D = 3.54

MP = 40

$$\text{Cost of equity capital (ke)} = \left[\frac{3.54}{40} + 0.10\right] \times 100$$

$$= (0.0885 + 0.10) \times 100$$

$$= 0.1885 \times 100 = 18.85\%$$

c. Cost of new equity shares (ke)

D = 3.54

NP = 40 – Floatation costs 5%

= 40 – (40 × 5%) = 40 – 2 = 38

$$ke = \left[\frac{D}{NP} + G\right] \times 100$$

$$= \left[\frac{3.54}{38} + 0.10\right] \times 100$$

$$= (0.0931 + 0.10) \times 100$$

$$= 0.193 \times 100 = 19.31$$

45. A Ltd. Intends to issue new equity shares. Its present equity shares are being sold in the market at Rs. 125 a share. The

company's past record regarding payment of dividends as follows.

1994-10.70%, 1995-11.45%, 1996-12.25%, 1997-13.11% and 1998-14.03%.

The floatation costs are estimated at 3% of the current selling price of the shares. You are required to calculate.

a. Growth rate in dividends.

b. Cost of funds raised by issue of equity shares assuming that the growth rate as calculated under above will continue for ever.

c. Cost of new equity shares.

Solution :

a. Growth rate in dividends (G)

During the 5 years from 1994-1998 dividend had increased from 10.70 to 14.03.

$$\text{The compound factor} = \frac{14.03}{10.70} = 1.311$$

In the compound factor table, the compound factor 1.311 in the row of 5 years is found in the 10% column. Hence the growth rate in dividend is 10%.

b. Cost of equity capital (Ke)

$$Ke = \left[\frac{D}{MP} + G\right] \times 100$$

D = Expectred Dividend = 14.030

Add: Growth (14.03 × 10%) = 1.403

D = 15.433

MP = 125

$$Ke = \left[\frac{15.433}{125} + 0.10\right] \times 100 = (0.123 + 0.10) \times 100$$

$$= 0.223 \times 100$$

$$= 22.30$$

c. Cost of new equity shares (Ke)

D = Expected Dividend = 15.433

NP = 125-Floatation Costs 3% = 125-3.75

= 121.25

$$Ke = \left[\frac{15.433}{121.25} + 0.10\right] \times 100 = (0.127 + 0.10) \times 100$$

$$= 0.227 \times 100$$

$$= 22.70\%$$

Earning Price Method

46. Blue star Ltd. is a dynamic growth firm. It pays no dividends and anticipates a long–run future earning of Rs. 7 per share. The current market price of the company's share is Rs. 55.45. Floatation costs for the issue of equity shares would be about 10% of the share price. What is the cost of new equity capital to Blue star?

Solution :

$$\text{Cost of Equity capital (Ke)} = \left[\frac{EPS}{NP}\right] \times 100$$

EPS = Earnings per share = Rs.7

Np = Issue price – Floatation costs 10%

$$= 55.45 - \left[55.45 \times \frac{10}{100}\right]$$

$$= 55.45 - 5.55 = 49.90$$

$$\text{Cost of Equity capital (ke)} = \left[\frac{7}{49.90}\right] \times 100 = 14.02\%$$

47. The entire capital of James Ltd. Consists of 5,00,000 shares of Rs.100 each. The profit after tax of the current year is rs.50,00,000. The company wants to raise Rs.2,00,00,000 by issuing new shares. The floatation costs are expected to be 10% of the face value of the shares.

    Calculate the cost of equity capital assuming that the earnings of the company are expected to be stable over the next 5 years.

Solution :

$$\text{Cost of Equity capital (Ke)} = \left[\frac{\text{EPS}}{\text{NP}}\right] \times 100$$

$$\text{EPS} = \frac{\text{Profit after tax}}{\text{No. of shares}} = \frac{50,00,000}{5,00,000} = \text{Rs.10.}$$

NP = Issue price – Floatation costs 10% = 100 – 10 = 90

$$\text{Cost of equity capital (Ke)} = \frac{10}{90} \times 100 = 11\%$$

48. Vijay Ltd. Wants to raise Rs.50,00,000 by the issue of new equity shares. The relevant information is given below:

No. of existing equity shares	= 10,00,000
Profit after tax	= Rs.60,00,000
Market value of existing shares	= Rs.4,00,00,000

a. Compute the cost of existing equity capital

b. Compute the cost of new capital if the shares are issued at a price of Rs.32 per share and the issue expenses are Rs. 2 per share.

Solution :

a. $\text{Cost of existing equity capital (Ke)} = \left[\frac{\text{EPS}}{\text{NP}}\right] \times 100$

$$\text{EPS} = \frac{\text{Profit after tax}}{\text{No. of shares}} = \frac{60,00,000}{10,00,000} = \text{Rs.6.}$$

$$\text{MP} = \text{Market price} = \left[\frac{\text{Market value}}{\text{No. of shares}}\right] = \frac{40,00,000}{10,00,000}$$

$$= \text{Rs.40}$$

$$\text{Cost of equity capital (Ke)} = \frac{6}{40} \times 100 = 15\%$$

b. Cost of new equity capital (Ke)

$$Ke = \frac{EPS}{NP} \times 100$$

NP = Issue Price – Expenses = 32-2 = Rs.30

$$\text{Cost of new equity capital Ke} = \frac{EPS}{NP} \times 100$$

$$= \frac{6}{30} \times 100 = 20\%$$

49. Snow Ltd. Earns a profit after tax of Rs.10,00,000. The company has 1,00,000 shares outstanding and the current market price per share is Rs.80. The earnings are expected to remain stable and the pay out is 100%.
   a. Calculate the cost of equity capital
   b. What will be the cost of equity capital if the pay our is 50% and the firm earns 15% on its investment?

Solution :

a. Cost of equity capital, when pay out is 100%

The pay out is 100% and earnings are expected to be stable. That is, no growth in earnings is anticipated. Hence, earnings – price method is used to calculate the cost of equity capital.

$$\text{Cost of equity capital (ke)} = \frac{EPS}{MP} \times 100$$

$$EPS = \frac{\text{Profit after tax}}{\text{No. of shares}} = \frac{10,00,000}{1,00,000} = \text{Rs.}10.$$

MP = 80

$$\text{Cost of equity capital (Ke)} = \frac{10}{80} \times 100 = 12.5\%$$

b. Cost of equity capital, when the pay out is 50%

$$\text{Cost of equity capital (ke)} = \left[\frac{D}{MP} + G\right] \times 100$$

$D = 10 \times 50\% = 5$

$MP = 80$

G = Retention Ratio × Expected Return = (100 – 50) × 15% = 50 × 15% = 7.5%

$$\text{Cost of equity capital (ke)} = \left[\frac{5}{80} + 0.075\right] \times 100$$

$$= (0.0625 + 0.075) \times 100$$

$$= 0.1375 \times 100 =$$

13.75%

Realised Yield Method

50. Rex Amalan purchased share in Royal Textiles Ltd., at Rs.317 per share, in January 2000. He held them for 5 years and sold them in January 2000 for Rs.500.

    The dividend per share received by he was as under:- 2000 – Rs. 15, 2001 – Rs. 15, 2002 – Rs. 18, 2003 – Rs. 18, 2004 – Rs. 20.

    Calculate the cost of equity capital.

    Under the realized yield method, cost of equity capital is the internal rate of return (IRR). It is the rate at which total present value of inflows to total present value of out flows. The IRR is calculated by trial and error.

Solution :

Calculated of present value of Inflows at 10% and 15%

Year	*Inflows Rs.*	*P.V. Factor at 10%*	*Present Values of Inflows at 10% Rs.*	*Inflows*	*P.V. Factor at 15%*	*Present Values of Inflows at 15% Rs.*
2000	15	0.909	13.635	15	0.870	13.050
2001	15	0826	12.390	15	0.756	11.340
2002	18	0.751	13.518	18	0.658	11.844
2003	18	0.683	12.294	18	0.572	10.296
2004	20	0.621	12.420	20	0.497	9.940
2005 (Sale Price)	500	0.564	282.00	500	0.432	216.000
Total	Present	Value	346.257			272.470

IRR is the rate at which total present value of inflows is equal to total present values of cash out flows. (NPV = 0). Present value of outflow = cost of the share = Rs.317

At 10% total present value of inflows = 346.257

At 15% total present value of inflows = 272.470

Decrease in Total present value = 73.787

The IRR lies between 10% and 15%

It is found as follows:

For a decrease of 73.787, increase in rate = 5% (15% - 10%).

For a decrease of 29.257, (346.257-317) increase in rate = $\frac{5}{73.787} \times 29.257 = 1.98$

Internal Rate of Return = 10 + 1.98 = 11.98%

At this rate, total present value of inflows = 317

cost of equity capital = IRR = 11.98%

Cost of Retained Earnings

51. A company's cost of equity capital (Ke) is 15%. The average tax rate of share holders is 40% and the brokerage cost for purchase of securities is 2%. Calculate the cost of retained earnings.

Solution :

Cost of equity capital (ke)	= 15.00
Less: Tax (15x40%)	= 6.00
	= 9.00
Less: Brokerage (9..00x2%)	= 0.18
Cost of Retained earnings	= 8.82

52. The followings particulars relate to Prakash Ltd. Equity share capital 1,00,000 shares of Rs. 10 = Rs. 10,00,000

    profit after tax = Rs.90,00,000

    current market price of Equity share = Rs.75

    a. Calculate the cost of equity.
    b. What is the cost of retained earnings if the average personal tax rate of share holders is 30% and the brokerage cost for making new investments is 2%.

Solution :

a. Cost of equity capital (ke) = $\frac{EPS}{MP} \times 100$

$$EPS = \frac{\text{Profit after tax}}{\text{No. of shares}} = \frac{90,00,000}{10,00,000} = Rs.9.$$

MP = Rs. 75

$$\text{Cost of equity capital (Ke)} = \frac{9}{75} \times 100 = 12\%$$

b. cost of retained earnings

Cost of equity capital (Ke)	= 12.00
Less: Tax (12.00x30%)	= 3.60
	= 8.40
Less: Brokerage (8.40x2%)	= 0.17
Cost of retained earnings (Ke)	= 8.23

53. Ajantha Ltd is earning a profit of Rs.1,00,000 P.a. The share holders required rate of return (Ke) is 10%. It is expected that if the earnings are distributed to the share holders, after paying taxes on dividends, they will invest the proceeds in the shares of similar firms and earn a 10% return. It is also estimated that the brokerage cost will be 2% of the investment what rate if return should be earned by the firm if the earnings are retained? Assume that the share holders are in 30% tax bracket?

Solution :

Particulars	*Rs.*
Profit available for distribution	1,00,000
Less: Income tax payable by share holders [1,00,000 × 30%]	30,000
Less: Brokerage on new investments	70,000
[70,000 × 2%]	1,400
Net amount available for Investment	6,860
[68,600 × 10%]	68,600
Rate of Return to be earned by the firm on Retained Earnings	
$Kr = \frac{6,860}{1,00,000} \times 100 = 6.86\%$	

WEIGHTED AVERAGE COST OF CAPITAL (WACC)

54. The capital structure and after tax cost of different sources of funds are given below.

Source of funds	*Amount Rs.*	*Proportion to total [W]*	*After tax cost % [X]*	*Weighted cost % [W] × [X]*
Equity share capital	4,00,000	0.40	14	5.60
Retained Earnings	2,00,000	0.20	13	2.60
Preference share capital	1,00,000	0.10	10	1.00
Debentures	3,00,000	0.30	6	1.80
Total	10,00,000		WACC	11.00

You are required to compute the weighted average cost of capital.

Solution :

Computation of Weighted Average Cost of Capital

Source of Funds	*Proportion to Total [W]*	*Cost % [x]*	*Weighted cost % = [W] × [X]*
Equity share capital	0.30	15	4.50
Retained Earnings	0.25	14	3.50
Preference share capital	0.20	10	2.00
Debentures	0.25	8	2.00
Weighted average cost of capital (WACC)			12.00

55. A firm finances all its investments by 60% equity and 40% debt. The estimated return on equity is 18% after taxes cost of debt is 8% after taxes. The firm is considering an investment proposal costing Rs.4,00,000 with an expected return that will continue for ever. What amount (in rupees) must the proposal yield per year so that at the market price of the share does not changes?

Solution :

Computation of weighted average cost of capital (WACC)

Source of Funds	*Proportion to Total [W]*	*Cost % [x]*	*Weighted cost % = [W] × [X]*
Equity	0.60	18	10.80
Debt	0.40	8	3.20
Weighted average cost of capital (WACC)			12.00
The investment must earn = 14% Earnings required = 4,00,000 × 14% = Rs. 56,000			

56. From the following particulars relating to the capital structure of blue ltd., calculated the overall cost of capital, using a. book value weights and b. market value weights.

Source of funds	*Book value (Bv)*	*Market value (MV)*
Equity share capital	45,000	90,000
Preference share capital	10,000	10,000
Debentures	30,000	30,000
Retained Earnings	15,000	-

The after tax cost of different sources finance is: Equity share capital 14%, Retained earnings 13% preference share capital 10%, Debentures 8%

Solution :

a. Computation of weighted average cost of captila (Book value weights)

Source of funds	*Amount Rs.*	*Proportion to total [W]*	*After tax cost % [X]*	*Weighted cost % [W] × [X]*
Equity share capital	40,00,000	0.500	17	8.500
Pref. Sh. Capital	10,00,000	0.125	6	0.750
Debentures	30,00,000	0.375	4	1.500
Total	80,00,000		WACC	10.750

b. Computation of weighted average cost of capital (Market value weights).

Source of funds	*Amount Rs.*	*Proportion to total [W]*	*After tax cost % [X]*	*Weighted cost % [W] × [X]*
Equity share capital	90,000	0.692	14	9.688
Preference share capital	10,000	0.077	10	0.770
Debentures	30,000	0.231	5	1.155
Total	1,30,000	WACC		11.613

Workings

Proportion refers to the proportion of each source to the total.

$$\frac{90000}{1,30,000} = 0.692, \frac{10,000}{1,30,000} = 0.077, \frac{30,000}{1,30,000} = 0.231$$

57. From the following capital structure of a company. Calculate the overall cost of capital

a. book value weight and

b. market value weight.

The after–tax cost of different source of finance is as follows:

Source of funds	*Book value (Bv)*	*Market value (MV)*	*Specified cost*
Equity share capital	60,000	1,20,000	13%
Retained Earnings	20,000	-	9%
Preference share capital	10,000	11,000	8%
Debentures	40,000	38,000	5%

Solution :

a. Computation of weighted average cost of capital (Book Value Weight)

Source of funds	*Amount Rs.*	*Proportion to total [W]*	*After tax cost % [X]*	*Weighted cost % [W] × [X]*
Debentures	40,000	0.308	5	1.540
Preference share capital	10,000	0.077	8	0.616
Equity share capital	60,000	0.462	13	6.006
Debentures	20,000	0.154	9	1.386
Total	1,30,000	WACC		9.548

b. Computation of weighted average cost of capital [Market value weight).

Source of funds	*Amount Rs.*	*Proportion to total [W]*	*After tax cost % [X]*	*Weighted cost % [W] × [X]*
Debentures	38,000	0.225	5	1.125
Preference share capital	11,000	0.065	8	0.520
Equity share capital	1,20,000	0.710	13	9.230
Total	1,69,000	WACC		10.875

Chapter 3

LEVERAGES

Meaning of Leverage

The dictionary meaning of the term leverage refers to an increased means for accomplishing some purpose.

For example, leverage helps as in lifting heavy objects, which may not be otherwise possible.

Definition of Leverage

James Horne has defined leverage as" the employment of an asset or funds for which the firm pays a fixed cost or fixed return.

Types of Leverages

Leverages are of three types:

1. Operating Leverage
2. financial Leverage
3. Composite Leverage

Operating Leverage

Meaning

The operating Leverage may be defined as the tendency of the operating profit to vary dis-proportionately with sales. It is said to exist when the firm has to pay fixed costs regardless of volume output or sales.

Operating leverage in a firm is a function of three factors.

i. The amount of fixed cost

ii. The contribution origin

iii. The volume of sales

$$\text{Degree of operating leverage} = \frac{\text{Contribution}}{\text{EBIT}}$$

Utility of Operating Leverage

The operating leverage indicates the impact of change in sales on operating income. If a firm has a high degree of operating leverage, a small change in sales will have a large effect on operating income.

Generally, the firms do not like to operate under conditions of a high degree of operating leverage. This is a very risky situation were a small drop in sales can be excessively damaging to the firms efforts to achieve profitability

FINANCIAL LEVERAGE OR TRADING ON EQUITY

Meaning

The financial leverage may be defined as the tendency of the residual net income to vary disproportionately with operating profit.

Favourable and Unfavourable Financial Leverages

Financial leverage may be favourable or unfavourable depending upon weather the earnings made by the use of fixed interest or dividend bearing securities exceed the explicit fixed cost, the firm has to pay for the employement of such funds. The leverage will be considered to be favourable so long the firm earns more on assets purchased with the funds than the fixed cost of their use. Unfavourable or negative leverage occurs when the firm does not earn as much as the funds cost.

Significance of Financial Leverage

1. *Planning of capital structure:* The capital structure is concerned with the raising of long term fund both from shareholders and long term creditors.

2. *Profit planning:* The earning per share is affected by the degree of financial leverage. If the profitability of to concern is increasing the fixed cost funds will help in increasing the availability of profits for equity shareholders.

Limitations of Financial Leverages

1. *Double–edged weapon:* Trading on equity is a double edged weapon. It can be successfully employed to increase the earnings of the share holders only when the rate of earnings of the company is more than the fixed rate of interest or dividend on debenture or preference shares.
2. *Beneficial only to companies having stability of earnings:* Trading on equity is beneficial only to the companies having stable and regular earnings.
3. *Increases risk and rate of interest:* Another limitation of trading on equity is on account of the fact that every rupee of extra debt increases the risk and hence the rate of interest on subsequent loans also goes on increasing.
4. *Restrictions from financial institutions:* The financial institutions also impose restrictions on companys which resort to excessive trading on equity because of the risk factor and to maintain a balance in the capital structure of the company.

5. *Composite leverage or combined leverage:*

$$\text{DCL} = \text{DOL} \times \text{DFl}$$

Practical Problems

i. $\text{Degree of Operating Leverage} = \dfrac{\text{Contribution}}{\text{EBIT}}$

ii. $\text{Degree of Financial Leverage} = \dfrac{\text{EBIT}}{\text{EBT}}$

iii. Degree of Combined Leverage = DOL × OFL

Sales	xxx
Less : Variable Cost	xxx
Contribution	xxx
Less : Fixed Cost	xxx
Earning Before Interest and Taxes (EBIT)	xxx
Less: Interest	xxx
Earning Before Tax (EBT)	xxx
Less : Taxes	xxx
Earning After Tax (EAT)	Xxx

1. Calculate the degree of operating leverage degree of financial leverage degree of combined leverage. From the following data:

   Sale 100000 units at Rs. 2 per unit

   Variable cost per unit at Rs. 0.80 per unit fixed cost Rs. 100000 Interest charges Rs. 4000

Solution :

Sales (100000 × 2)	200000
Less : Variable Cost (100000 × 0.80)	80000
Contribution	120000
Less : Fixed Cost	100000
EBIT	20000
Less: Interest	4000
EBT	16000

1. $DOL = \frac{Contribution}{EBIT} = \frac{120000}{20000} = 6$

2. $DFL = \frac{EBIT}{EBT} = \frac{20000}{16000} = 1.25$

3. $DCL = DOL \times DFL = 6 \times 1.25 = 7.50$

2. Calculate the DOL, DFL and DCL for the following firms and interpret the result.

Particulars	*P*	*Q*	*R*
Output units	300000	75000	500000
Fixed costs (Rs)	350000	700000	75000
Variable cost per unit (Rs)	1.00	7.50	0.10
Interest charges (Rs)	25000	40000	-
Selling price per unit	3.00	25.00	0.50

Solution :

Particulars	*P*	*Q*	*R*
Sales (units × price) (300000 × 3) (75000 × 25) (500000 × 0.50)	900000	1875000	250000
Less: Variable Cost (unit × price) (300000 × 1) (75000 × 7.50)(500000 × 0.10)	300000	562500	50000
Contribution	600000	1312500	200000
Less : Fixed Cost	350000	700000	75000
EBIT	250000	612500	125000
Less : Interest	25000	40000	-
EBT	225000	572500	125000

Firm – P

1. $DOL = \frac{\text{Contribution}}{\text{EBIT}} = \frac{600000}{250000} = 2.4$

2. $DFL = \frac{\text{EBIT}}{\text{EBT}} = \frac{250000}{225000} = 1.11$

3. DCL = DOL × DFL = 2.4 × 1.11 = 2.67

Firm – Q

1. $DOL = \frac{\text{Contribution}}{\text{EBIT}} = \frac{1312500}{612500} = 2.14$

2. $DFL = \frac{\text{EBIT}}{\text{EBT}} = \frac{612500}{572500} = 1.06$

3. DCL = DOL × DFL = 2.14 × 1.06 = 2.26

Firm – R

1. $DOL = \frac{\text{Contribution}}{\text{EBIT}} = \frac{200000}{125000} = 1.6$

2. $DFL = \frac{EBIT}{EBT} = \frac{125000}{125000} = 1$

3. $DCL = DOL \times DFL = 1.6 \times 1 = 1.6$

3. Calculate leverages from the following

   Production (Units) - 75000
   Fixed Exp's - 700000
   Variable Cost (unit) - 7.50
   Interest Exp's - 40000
   Selling price (units) - 25

Solution :

Sales (75000 × 25)	1875000
Less: Variable Cost (75000 × 7.50)	562500
Contribution	1312500
Less: Fixed Cost	700000
(EBIT)	612500
Less: Interest	40000
(EBT)	572500

1. $DOL = \frac{Contribution}{EBIT} = \frac{1312500}{612500} = 2.14$

2. $DFL = \frac{EBIT}{EBT} = \frac{612500}{372500} = 1.069$

3. $DCL = DOL \times DFL = 2.14 \times 1.069 = 2.29$

4. The following figures relate to a companies

Particulars	*P*	*Q*
Sales	500000	1000000
Variable cost	200000	300000
Contribution	300000	700000
Fixed cost	150000	400000
EBIT	150000	300000
Interest	50000	100000
Profit Before Tax (EBT)	100000	200000

Calculate operating, financial and composite leverage.

Solution :

Firm – P

1. $DOL = \frac{Contribution}{EBIT} = \frac{300000}{150000} = 2$

2. $DFL = \frac{EBIT}{EBT} = \frac{150000}{100000} = 1.5$

3. $DCL = DOL \times DFL = 2 \times 1.5 = 3$

Firm – Q

1. DOL = = = 2.3

2. DFL = = = 1.5

3. $DCL = DOL \times DFL = 2.3 \times 1.5 = 3.45$

5. Find the Financial Leverage from the following data:

   Net worth = 2500000

   Debt Equity = 3 : 1

   Interest rate = 12%

   Operating income = 2000000

Solution :

EBIT	2000000
Less: Interest (2500000 × 12/100)	300000
EBT	1700000

$$\text{Financial Leverage} = \frac{EBIT}{EBT}$$

$$= \frac{2000000}{1700000} = 1.18$$

6. A firm manufactures and sales 5000 units of product be selling price per unit is Rs. 30 and variable cost per unit is Rs.20 if the EBIT is Rs.30000 what are its fixed cost?

Solution :

Sales (5000 × 30)	150000
Less : Variable cost (5000 × 20)	100000
Contribution	50000
Less : Fixed cost	20000
EBIT	30000

7. What is the EBIT for each of the following data sets
   a. P = Rs.10 Q = 20000 V = Rs 6 F= 50000
   b. P = Rs.50 Q = 12000 V = Rs 30 F= 200000

Solution :

(a) Sales (20000 × 10)	200000
Less : Variable cost (20000 × 6)	120000
Contribution	80000
Less : Fixed cost	50000
EBIT	30000
(b) Sales (12000 × 50)	600000
Less : Variable cost (12000 × 30)	360000
Contribution	240000
Less : Fixed cost	200000
EBIT	40000

8. Calculate the operating leverage ratio. For each of the 4 firms A, B, C and D from the following price and cost data for the purpose of your calculations use a level of sales of 5000 units in each case what conclusion which respect to level of fixed cost and the degree of operating result. DOL

Particulars	*A*	*B*	*C*	*D*
Sales price per unit (Rs)	20	32	50	70
Variable cost per unit (Rs)	6	16	20	50
Fixed operating cost (Rs)	80000	40000	200000	-

Solution :

(a) Sales (5000 × 20)	100000
Less : Variable cost (5000 × 6)	30000
Contribution	70000
Less : Fixed cost	80000
EBIT	10000

1. $$DOL = \frac{Contribution}{EBIT} = \frac{70000}{10000} = 7$$

(b) Sales (5000 × 32)	160000
Less: Variable cost (5000 × 16)	80000
Contribution	80000
Less: Fixed cost	40000
EBIT	40000

1. $$DOL = \frac{Contribution}{EBIT} = \frac{80000}{40000} = 2$$

(c) Sales (5000 × 50)	250000
Less: Variable cost (5000 × 20)	100000
Contribution	150000
Less: Fixed cost	200000
EBIT	50000

1. $$DOL = \frac{Contribution}{EBIT} = \frac{150000}{50000} = 3$$

(d) Sales (5000 × 70)	350000
Less : Variable cost (5000 × 50)	250000
Contribution	100000
Less : Fixed cost	-
EBIT	100000

1. $$DOL = \frac{Contribution}{EBIT} = \frac{100000}{100000} = 1$$

9. Determine the break even point for the following firms

Particulars	*X*	*Y*	*Z*
Sales price per unit (Rs.)	90	60	20
Variable cost per unit (Rs.)	60	18	10
Fixed operating cost (Rs.)	300000	420000	200000

Solution :

$$BEP = \frac{Fixed\,Cost}{P.V.R}$$

$$PVR = \frac{\text{Contribution}}{\text{Sales}} \times 100$$

	X	*Y*	*Z*
Sales price Per unit	90	60	20
Less : Variable Cost per unit	60	18	10
Contribution	30	42	10

$$P.V.R = \frac{\text{Contribution}}{\text{Sales}} \times 100 = \frac{30}{90} \times 100 = \frac{42}{60} \times 100 = \frac{10}{20} \times 100$$

$$= 33.33\% \quad = 70\% \quad = 50\%$$

$$B.E.P. = \frac{F.C.}{P.V.R} = \frac{300000}{33/100} \qquad = \frac{420000}{70/100} \qquad = \frac{200000}{50/100}$$

$$= 30000 \times {}^{100}\!/_{33} = 420000 \times {}^{100}\!/_{70} = 200000 \times {}^{100}\!/_{50}$$

$$= 909.090 \qquad 600000 \qquad 400000$$

10. Calculate operating leverage and financial leverage under situations A, B and C and financial plans 1, 2 and 3 respectively. From the following informations relating to the operation and capital structure of xyz company also find out the combinations of operating and financial leverage which gives the highest value and least value how are these calculations useful to the financial manager of a company?

    Installed capacity 1200 units

    Actual production and sales 800 units

    Selling price per units Rs. 15

    Variable cost per units Rs. 10

    Fixed Cost

    Situation A : Rs.1000

    Situation B : Rs. 2000

    Situation C : Rs. 3000

Solution :

Capital structure: *Financial Plans*

Particulars	*1*	*2*	*3*
Equity Rs.	5000	7500	2500
Debt Rs.	5000	2500	7500
Cost of Debt (For all plans)		12%	

Determination of Operating Leverage

Particulars	*A*	*B*	*C*
Sales (unit x selling price P.U 800 x 15)	12000	12000	12000
Less : Variable Cost (800 x 10)	8000	8000	8000
Contribution	4000	4000	4000
Less : Fixed Cost	1000	2000	3000
EBIT	3000	2000	1000

A. $DOL = \frac{C}{EBIT} = \frac{4000}{3000} = 1.33$

B. $DOL = \frac{C}{EBIT} = \frac{4000}{2000} = 2$

C. A. $DOL = \frac{C}{EBIT} = \frac{4000}{1000} = 4$

Determination of Financial Leverage

Situation – A *Financial plan*

Particulars	*1*	*2*	*3*
EBIT	3000	3000	3000
Less : Interest, 5000 × 12/100, 2500 × 12/100, 7500 × 12/100	600	300	900
EBT	2400	2700	2100

1. $DFL = \frac{EBIT}{EBT} = \frac{3000}{2400} = 1.25$

2. $DFL = \frac{EBIT}{EBT} = \frac{3000}{2700} = 1.1$

3. $\text{DFL} = \dfrac{\text{EBIT}}{\text{EBT}} = \dfrac{3000}{2700} = 1.43$

Situation–B *Financial plan*

Particulars	*1*	*2*	*3*
EBIT	2000	2000	2000
Less: Interest	600	300	900
EBT	1400	1700	1100

1. $\text{DFL} = \dfrac{\text{EBIT}}{\text{EBT}} = \dfrac{2000}{1400} = 1.42$
2. $\text{DFL} = \dfrac{\text{EBIT}}{\text{EBT}} = \dfrac{2000}{1700} = 1.18$
3. $\text{DFL} = \dfrac{\text{EBIT}}{\text{EBT}} = \dfrac{2000}{1100} = 1.83$

Situation–C *Financial plan*

Particulars	*1*	*2*	*3*
EBIT	2000	2000	2000
Less: Interest	600	300	900
EBT	400	700	100

1. $\text{DFL} = \dfrac{\text{EBIT}}{\text{EBT}} = \dfrac{1000}{400} = 2.5$
2. $\text{DFL} = \dfrac{\text{EBIT}}{\text{EBT}} = \dfrac{1000}{700} = 1.43$
3. $\text{DFL} = \dfrac{\text{EBIT}}{\text{EBT}} = \dfrac{1000}{100} = 10$

Degree of Combined Leverage = DOL × DFL

Situation *Financial plan*

	1	2	3
A	1.33 × 1.25 = 1.66	1.33 × 1.11 = 1.48	1.33 × 1.43 = 1.48
B	2 × 1.43 = 2.86	2 × 1.18 = 2.36	2 × 1.82 = 3.64
C	4 × 2.50 = 10	4 × 1.43 = 5.72	4 × 10 = 40

11. The Capital structure of the progressive corporation consist of an ordinary share capital of Rs.1000000 (shares of Rs. 100 per value) and Rs. 1000000 of 10% debentures sales increased by 20% from 100000 units to 120000 units. The selling price is Rs. 10 per unit. Variable cost amount to Rs. 6 per unit and fixed exp's amount to Rs. 200000 the income tax rate is assumed to be 50%.

    You are required to calculate the following (i) The percentage increase in earning per shares (EPS) (ii) The Degree of financial leverage at 100000 units and 120000 units (iii) The degree of operating leverage at 100000 units and 120000 units.

Solution :

Particulars	*100000 units*	*120000 units*
Sales (100000 x 10) (120000 x 10)	1000000	1200000
Less : Variable Cost (100000x6) (120000x6)	600000	720000
Contribution	400000	480000
Less : Fixed Cost	200000	200000
EBIT	200000	280000
Less : Interest(1000000x10/100)	100000	100000
EBT	100000	180000
Less : Tax 50%	50000	90000
EAT	50000	90000
No. of Equity Shares (N)	10000	10000
$\left[\frac{1000000}{100}\right]$ EPS $\left[\frac{EAT}{N}\right]$	5	9

1. The % increase in EPS = $\frac{\Delta EPS}{EPS}$ = 4/5 × 100 = 80%

   Δ EPS = 9 – 5 = 4

2. DFL = $\frac{EBIT}{EBT}$ at 100000 units = $\frac{200000}{100000}$ = 2

   at 120000 units $\frac{280000}{180000}$ = 1.56

3. DOL $\frac{C}{EBIT}$ at 100000 units = $\frac{400000}{200000} = 2$

at 120000 units = $\frac{480000}{280000} = 1.71$

12. The hardware company ltd has to make a choice between debt issue and equity for each expansion programme. Its current. Position is as follows.

Particulars	*Rs.*
5% debt	20000
Equity capital (Rs. 10 per share)	50000
Surplus	30000
Total capitalization	100000
Sales	300000
Total cost	296000
Income before interest & taxes (or) EBIT	31000
Less : Interest	1000
EBT	30000
Less : Income Tax	15000
EAT	15000

The expansion programme is estimated to cost Rs.50000 if this financed through debt. The rate on new debt will be 7% and the price earning ratio will be 6 times it the expansion programme. Financed through equity new shares can be sold netting Rs.25 per share and the price earning ratio will be 7 times. The expansion will generate additional sales of 150000 with a return of 10% on sales before interest and taxes.

If the company is to follow a policy of maximizing the market value of its share which from of financing should it choose ?

Solution :

Workings

1. *EBIT:*

Present EBIT 31000

(+) Expected EBIT
(150000 × 10/100) 15000
46000

2. *EPS:* Indebt financing the number of ordinary shares out standing would remained unchanged that is 5000 (50000/ 10). However in the case of equity form of financing this figure will go up by 2000 (50000/25) that is new equity share issued determination of market value of share.

Particulars		*Financial plan*
	7% debt	Equity issue
EBIT	46000	46000
Less : Interest 50000 × 7/100	4500	1000
= 35003500 + 1000		
EBT	41500	45000
Less : Income Tax 50 %	20750	22500
EAT	20750	22500
EPS $\left[\frac{\text{EAT}}{\text{N}}\right]$	4.15	3.214
$\frac{20750}{5000}, \frac{22500}{7000}(5000+2000)$		
Price earning ratio (PE ratio)	6 times	7 times
Market value of share	24.90	22.50
EPS × PE ratio	4.15 × 6	3.214 × 7

The company should choose debt form of financing to maximize the market value of its shares.

13. The well established company's most recent B/S is as follows.

Liabilities		*Assets*	
Share Capital (10 per share)	60000	Net Fixed Assets	150000
10% long term debt	80000	Current Assets	50000
Retained Earnings	20000		
Current Liabilities	40000		
	200000		200000

The companies total assets turnover ratio is 3 is fixed operating cost are Rs.100000 and its variable operating cost ratio 40%. The income tax ratio is 50%.

1. Calculate for the company all the three types of leverage
2. Defer the likely level of EBIT if EPS is (A) Re.1 (B) Rs. 3 (C) Zero

Solution :
Working:

$$\text{Total assets turnover ratio} = \frac{\text{Sales}}{\text{Total Assets}}$$

$$3 = \frac{\text{Sales}}{\text{Total Assets}}$$

$$3 = \frac{\text{Sales}}{2,00,000}$$

$$200000 \times 3 = \text{Sales}$$

$$\text{Sales} = 600000$$

2. Interest = 80000 × 10/100 = 8000

(a) Income statement of the company :-

Particulars	*Amount*
Sales	600000
Less: Variable Cost (600000 × 40/100)	240000
Contribution	360000
Less: Fixed Cost	100000
EBIT	260000
Less: Interest	8000
EBT	252000
Less: Taxes 252000 × 50/100	126000
EAT	126000

$$\text{(A) DOL} = \frac{C}{\text{EBIT}} = \frac{360000}{260000} = 1.38$$

$$\text{(B) DFL} = \frac{\text{EBIT}}{\text{EBT}} = \frac{260000}{252000} = 1.03$$

$$\text{(C) DCL} = \text{DOL} \times \text{DFL} = 1.38 \times 1.03 = 1.42$$

2. (a) $EPS = \frac{(EBIT - Interest)(1 - Tax)}{Number\ of\ shares}$

$$N = \frac{60000}{10} = 6000$$

(a) $1 = \frac{(EBIT - 8000)(1 - 0.50)}{6000}$

$6000 = (EBIT - 8000)\ 0.50$

$6000 = 0.50\ EBIT - 4000$

$-0.5\ EBIT = -4000 - 6000$

$-0.5\ EBIT = -10000$

$$EBIT = \frac{10000}{0.5} = 20000$$

(b) $3 = \frac{(EBIT - 8000)(1 - 0.5)}{6000}$

$18000 = (EBIT - 8000)\ 0.5$

$18000 = 0.5\ EBIT - 4000$

$-0.5\ EBIT = -4000 - 18000$

$-0.5\ EBIT = -22000$

EBIT =

(c) $0 = \frac{(EBIT - 8000)(1 - 0.50)}{6000}$

$0 = (EBIT - 8000)\ 0.5$

$0 = 0.5\ EBIT - 4000$

$-0.5\ EBIT = -4000$

$$EBIT = \frac{4000}{0.5} = 8000$$

Confirmation Table

EBIT	20000	44000	8000
Less: Interest	8000	8000	8000
EBT	12000	36000	-
Less : Tax 50%	6000	18000	-
EAT	6000	18000	-
No. of Shares (N)	6000	6000	6000

EPS (EAT/N) $\frac{6000}{6000} = 1$ $\frac{18000}{6000} = 3$ $\frac{0}{6000} = 0$

14. Calculate the level of EBIT at which the indifferent point between the following financing alternative will accure.
    1. Common share capital of Rs.1000000 and 8%debentures of Rs. 50000 and common share capital of Rs.500000.
    2. Common Share capital of Rs. 1000000 and 8% preference share capital of Rs. 500000 and common share capital of Rs. 500000.
    3. Common share capital of Rs. 1000000 and common share capital of Rs. 500000 8%. Preference share capital of Rs. 200000 and 8% debentures of Rs. 300000.
    4. Common share capital of Rs.600000 and 6% debentures of Rs.400000 and common share capital of Rs. 400000 8% preference share capital of Rs. 200000 and 6% debentures of Rs. 400000.
    5. Common share capital of Rs. 600000 and 6% preference share capital of Rs. 400000 and common share capital of Rs. 400000 6% preference share capital of Rs.200000 and 8% debentures of Rs. 400000.

Solution :

Assume that the price of a common share is Rs.10 each case and tax rate is 50%. The different points for the various combinations of the methods of finance are calculated as follows

$$1. = \frac{(1-T)EBIT}{N_1} = \frac{(1-T)(EBIT-l)}{N_2}$$

$$2. = \frac{(1-T)EBIT}{N_1} = \frac{(1-T)(EBIT-D)}{N_2}$$

$$3. = \frac{(1-T)EBIT}{N_1} = \frac{(1-T)(EBIT-l)-D}{N_2}$$

$$4. = \frac{(1-T)(EBIT-l_1)}{N_1} = \frac{(1-T)(EBIT-l_2)-D}{N_2}$$

5. $$= \frac{(1-T)(EBIT - D_1)}{N_1} = \frac{(1-T)(EBIT - I) - D_2}{N_2}$$

1. $$\frac{(1-T)EBIT}{N_1} = \frac{(1-T)(EBIT - I)}{N_2}$$

$$\frac{(1-0.50)EBIT}{100000} = \frac{(1-0.50)(EBIT - 40000)}{50000}$$

$$\frac{0.50\,EBIT}{100000} = \frac{0.50(EBIT - 40000)}{50000}$$

$$0.5\ EBIT = (0.5\ EBIT - 20000)$$

$$0.5\ EBIT = 2(0.5EBIT - 20000)$$

$$0.5EBIT = EBIT - 40000$$

$$-EBIT + 0.5\ EBIT = -40000$$

$$-0.5\ EBIT = -40000$$

$$EBIT = \frac{40000}{0.5} = 80000$$

$$\therefore \quad EBIT = 80000$$

2. $$\frac{(1-T)EBIT}{N_1} = \frac{(1-T)(EBIT - D)}{N_2}$$

$$\frac{(1-0.50)EBIT}{100000} = \frac{(1-0.50)(EBIT - 40000)}{50000}$$

$$0.5\ EBIT = \frac{1,00,000}{50,000}(0.5\ EBIT - 20000)$$

$$0.5\ EBIT = 2(0.5EBIT - 20000)$$

$$0.5EBIT = EBIT - 40000$$

$$0.5\ EBIT - EBIT = -40000$$

$$-0.5\ EBIT = -40000$$

$$EBIT = \ = 80000$$

$$\therefore \quad EBIT = 80000$$

3. $$\frac{(1-T)EBIT}{N_1} = \frac{(1-T)(EBIT - I) - D}{N_2}$$

$$\frac{(1-0.50)\text{EBIT}}{100000} = \frac{(1-0.50)(\text{EBIT}-24000)-16000}{50000}$$

0.5EBIT = 2(0.5 EBIT – 28000)

0.5 EBIT = EBIT – 56000

– 0.5 EBIT = – 56000

EBIT = 112000

4. $$\frac{(1-T)(\text{EBIT}-I_1)}{N_1} = \frac{(1-T)(\text{EBIT}-I_2)-D}{N_2}$$

$$= \frac{(1-0.50)(\text{EBIT}-24000)}{60000}$$

$$= \frac{(1-0.50)(\text{EBIT}-24000)-16000}{40000}$$

0.5 EBIT – 12000 = (0.5 EBIT – 12000 – 16000)

0.5 EBIT – 12000 = 1.5 (0.5EBIT – 28000)

0.5 EBIT = 0.75 EBIT – 42000 + 12000

0.5 EBIT – 0.75 EBIT = – 30000

– 0.25 EBIT = – 30000

EBIT = = 1,20000

5. $$\frac{(1-T)(\text{EBIT}-D_1)}{N_1} = \frac{(1-T)(\text{EBIT}-I)-D_2}{N_2}$$

$$\frac{(1-0.50)(\text{EBIT}-24000)}{60000}$$

$$= \frac{(1-0.50)(\text{EBIT}-320000)-12000}{40000}$$

0.5 EBIT –12000 = 1.5 (0.5 EBIT – 28000)

0.5 EBIT – 0.75 EBIT = – 42000 +12000

0.5 EBIT – 0.75 EBIT = – 30000

– 0.25 EBIT = – 30000

EBIT = = 1,20000

15. Calculate the level of EBIT at which the indifference point between the following financing alternative will acquire.

i. Common share capital of Rs.1000000 of 15% debentures of Rs.500000 and common share capital at Rs.500000.

ii. Common share capital of Rs.1000000 of 13% preference share capital of Rs.500000 and common share capital of Rs.500000.

iii. Common share capital of Rs.1000000 common share capital of Rs. 500000 13%. Preference share capital of Rs. 2,00,000 and 15% debentures of Rs.3,00,000.

iv. Common share capital of Rs.600000 and 15% debentures of Rs.400000 or common share capital of Rs.200000 and 15% debentures of Rs.400000.

v. Common share capital of Rs.500000 and 13% preference share capital of Rs.200000 or common share capital of Rs.400000 13% preference share capital of Rs.200000 15% debentures of Rs.400000.

Solution :

Assume that the corporate tax rate is 50% and the price of the common share is Rs.10 in each cash.

1. $$\frac{(1-T)EBIT}{N_1} = \frac{(1-T)(EBIT-1)}{N_2}$$

$$\frac{(1-0.50)EBIT}{100000} = \frac{(1-0.50)(EBIT-75000)}{50000}$$

$$\frac{0.50\,EBIT}{100000} = \frac{(0.50)(EBIT-75000)}{50000}$$

$$0.50\ EBIT = \frac{100000}{50000}(0.5\ EBIT - 37500)$$

$$0.50\ EBIT = 2(0.5EBIT - 37500)$$

$$0.50\ EBIT = EBIT - 75000$$

$$0.50\ EBIT - EBIT = -75000$$

$$-0.5EBIT = -75000$$

$$EBIT = \frac{75000}{0.5} = 150000$$

(2) $$\frac{(1-T)\text{EBIT}}{N_1} = \frac{(1-T)(\text{EBIT}-D)}{N_2}$$

$$\frac{(1-0.50)\text{EBIT}}{100000} = \frac{(1-0.50)(\text{EBIT}-65000)}{50000}$$

$$0.5\ \text{EBIT} = (0.5\text{EBIT} - 32500)$$

$$0.5\text{EBIT} = \text{EBIT} - 65000$$

$$0.5\ \text{EBIT} - \text{EBIT} = -65000$$

$$-0.5\ \text{EBIT} = -65000$$

$$\text{EBIT} = \frac{65000}{0.5} = 130000$$

$$\therefore\ \text{EBIT} = 130000$$

(3) $$\frac{(1-T)\text{EBIT}}{N_1} = \frac{(1-T)(\text{EBIT}-I)-D}{N_2}$$

$$\frac{(1-0.50)\text{EBIT}}{100000} = \frac{(1-0.50)(\text{EBIT}-45000)-26000}{50000}$$

$$0.5\ \text{EBIT} = \frac{100000}{50000}\ (0.5\text{EBIT} - 22500\text{-}26000)$$

$$0.5\ \text{EBIT} = \text{EBIT} - 97000$$

$$-0.5\ \text{EBIT} = -97000$$

$$\text{EBIT} = \frac{97000}{0.5} = 194000$$

$$\therefore\ \text{EBIT} = 194000$$

(4) $$\frac{(1-T)(\text{EBIT}-I_1)}{N_1} = \frac{(1-T)(\text{EBIT}-I_2)-D}{N_2}$$

$$\frac{(1-0.50)(\text{EBIT}-60000)}{60000}$$

$$= \frac{(1-0.50)(\text{EBIT}-60000)-26000}{40000}$$

$$0.5 \text{ EBIT} - 30000 = (0.5 \text{ EBIT} - 30000 - 26000)$$

$$0.5 \text{ EBIT} - 30000 = 1.5\ (0.5\text{EBIT} - 56000)$$

$$0.5 \text{ EBIT} = 0.75 \text{ EBIT} - 84000 + 30000$$

$$0.5 \text{ EBIT-}0.75 \text{ EBIT} = -54000$$

$$-0.25 \text{ EBIT} = -54000$$

$$\text{EBIT} = \frac{54000}{0.25} = 216000$$

(5) $$\frac{(1-T)(\text{EBIT}-D_1)}{N_1} = \frac{(1-T)(\text{EBIT}-I)D-D_2}{N_2}$$

$$\frac{(1-0.50)(\text{EBIT}-26000)}{80000}$$

$$= \frac{(1-0.50)(\text{EBIT}-60000)-26000}{40000}$$

$$0.5 \text{ EBIT} - 13000 = (0.5 \text{ EBIT} - 30000 - 26000)$$

$$0.5 \text{ EBIT} - 13000 = 2\ (0.5 \text{ EBIT} - 56000)$$

$$0.5 \text{ EBIT} = \text{EBIT} - 112000 + 13000$$

$$0.5 \text{ EBIT} - \text{EBIT} = -99000$$

$$-0.5 \text{ EBIT} = -99000$$

$$\text{EBIT} = \frac{99000}{5} = 198000$$

16. Pradhan Enterprises is currently selling 400 units per year. If the selling price per unit is Rs.1000 and variable cost per unit is Rs.600 and fixed costs are Rs.1,00,000 what is Pradhan's DOL at its current level of operations ? what will be the DOL if the quantity sold rises to 600 units?

Solution :

Determination of Operating Leverage.

Sales (400 × 1000)	4,00,000
Less: variable cost (400 × 600)	2,40,000
Contribution	1,60,000
Less: Fixed costs	1,00,000
EBIT	60,000

$$DOL = \frac{Contribution}{EBIT} = \frac{1,60,000}{4,00,000} = 0.40$$

Sales (600 × 1000)	6,00,000
Less: Variable cost (600 × 600)	3,60,000
Contribution	2,40,000
Less: Fixed Cost	1,00,000
EBIT	1,40,000

$$DOL = \frac{Contribution}{EBIT} = \frac{2,40,000}{6,00,000} = 0.60$$

17. Consider the following data for sylex company:

Unit Selling Price	Rs. 60
Unit Variable Cost	Rs. 40
Total fixed costs	Rs. 3,00,000
Interest burden	Rs. 1,00,000
Tax rate	= 50%
Preference dividend	Rs. 50,000

What is the degree of financial leverage (DFL) when the EBIT are Rs.4,00,000? What percentage change would occure in the EPS if EBIT increases by 10%?

Solution :

Determination of Financial Leverage

EBIT	4,00,000	4,00,000
Add: Increase 10% of EBIT	-	40,000
$(4,00,000 \times \frac{10}{100})$		
Revised EBIT	4,00,000	4,40,000
Less: Interest	1,00,000	1,00,000
EBT	3,00,000	3,40,000
Less : Tax 50%	1,50,000	1,70,000
EAT	1,50,000	1,70,000
DFL =	$\frac{4,00,000}{3,00,000} = 1.33$	$\frac{4,40,000}{3,40,000} = 1.29$
Preference share (N)	50,000	50,000
EPS = EAT/N	$\frac{1,50,000}{50,000} = 3$	$\frac{1,70,000}{50,000} = 3.4$

$$\text{Percentage Increase in EPS} = \frac{\Delta EPS}{EPS} \times 100$$

$$\Delta EPS = 3.4 - 3 = 0.4$$

$$= \frac{0.40}{3} \times 100 = 13\%$$

18. The operating and cost debts of Ashock Ltd are as follows:

    Sales 40,000 units at Rs.10 per unit.

    Variable cost at Rs.7.50 per unit.

    Fixed costs Rs.80,000 (including 15% interest on Rs.2,00,000).

    Calculate the operating, financial and combined leverage.

Solution:

Statement of Profit

Sales (40,000 × 10)	4,00,000
Less: Variable cost (40,000 × 7.50)	3,00,000
Contribution	1,00,000
Less: Fixed cost (80,000 – (2,00,000 × 15%))(80,000 × 30,000)	50,000
EBIT	50,000
Less: Interest	30,000
EBT	20,000

1. $\text{DOL} = \dfrac{\text{Contribution}}{\text{EBIT}} = \dfrac{1{,}00{,}000}{50{,}000} = 2$

2. $\text{DFL} = \dfrac{\text{EBIT}}{\text{EBT}} = \dfrac{50{,}000}{20{,}000} = 2.5$

3. DCL = DOL × DFL = 2 × 2.5 = 5.

19. Calculate operating and financial leverages from the following particulars.

    Units sold 5,000

    Variable cost per unit Rs. 20

    Selling price per unit Rs. 30

    10% public debt Rs. 1,00,000

    EBIT Rs. 30,000.

Statement of Profit

Sales (5,0000 × 3)	1,50,000
Less: Variable cost (50,000 × 20)	1,00,000
Contribution	50,000
Less: Fixed cost	20,000
EBIT	30,000
Less: Interest (1,00,000 × 10%)	10,000
EBT	20,000

a. Operating Leverage = $\frac{\text{Contribution}}{\text{EBIT}}$

$$= \frac{50,000}{30,000} = 1.67$$

b. Financial Leverage = $\frac{\text{EBIT}}{\text{EBT}} = \frac{30,000}{20,000} = 1.50$

20. Calculate operating leverage for maruthi led., from the following information:

No. of units produced	Rs. 50,000
Selling price per unit	Rs. 50
Variable cost per unit	Rs. 20

Fixed cost per unit at current level of sales Rs. 15. What will be the new operating leverage, if the variable cost is Rs.30 per unit.

Solution :

Statement of Profit

Sales (50,000 × 50)	25,00,000
Less: Variable cost (50,000 × 20)	10,00,000
Contribution	15,00,000
Less: Fixed cost (50,000 × 15)	7,50,000
EBIT	7,50,000

Operating Leverage = $\frac{\text{Contribution}}{\text{EBIT}}$

$$\frac{15,00,000}{7,50,000} = 2$$

New operating leverage if variable cost is Rs. 30 per unit

Sales (50,000 × 50)	25,00,000
Less: Variable cost (50,000 × 30)	15,00,000
Contribution	10,00,000
Less: Fixed cost	7,50,000
EBIT	2,50,000

$$\text{Operating Leverage} = \frac{10,00,000}{2,50,000} = 4$$

21. The following projections have been given in respect of companies x and y.

Particulars	*Company X*	*Company Y*
Volume of output and sales	80,000 units	1,00,000 units
Variable cost per unit	Rs.4	Rs.3
Fixed Cost	Rs.2,40,000	Rs.2,50,000
Interest burden on debt	Rs.1,20,000	Rs.50,000
Selling Price Per Unit	Rs.10	Rs.8

On the basis of above information calculate a. Operating leverage, b. Financial leverage, c. Combined leverage, d. Operating break even point e. Financial break even point.

Solution :

Statement of profit

	Company X	*Company Y*
Sales (80,000 × 10, 1,00,000 × 8)	8,00,000	8,00,000
Less: Variable cost (80,00 × 4, 1,00,000 × 3)	3,20,000	3,00,000
Contribution	4,80,000	5,00,000
Less: Fixed cost	2,40,000	2,50,000
EBIT	2,40,000	2,50,000
Less: Interest	1,20,000	50,000
EBT	1,20,000	2,00,000
a. Operating Leverage $\frac{\text{Contribution}}{\text{EBIT}}$	$\frac{4,80,000}{2,40,000} = 2$	$\frac{5,00,000}{2,50,000} = 2$
b. Financial Leverage	$\frac{2,40,000}{1,20,000} = 2$	$\frac{2,60,000}{2,00,000} = 1.25$

Contd...

$\frac{\text{EBIT}}{\text{EBT}}$		
c. Combined Leverage = DOL x DFL	$2 \times 2 = 4$	$2 \times 1.25 = 2.50$
d. Operating B.E. P units	$\frac{2,40,000}{6}$	$\frac{2,50,000}{5}$
$\frac{\text{Fiexd Cost}}{\text{Contribution Perunit}}$	= 40,000 units	= 50,000 units
e. financial B.E.P units	$\frac{2,40,000}{6} \times 10$	$\frac{2,50,000}{5} \times 8$
Selling Price Per unit	= 4,00,000 units	= 4,00,000

22. The capital structure of Bata Ltd. Consists of Equity share capital of Rs.1,00,000 and 8% debentures of Rs.50,000. The fixed costs Rs.10,000. You are required to calculate the operating and Financial leverages where earnings before interest and taxes is Rs.20,000.

Solution :

a. Operating Leverage =

contribution = Fixed cost + EBIT

= 10,000+20,000 = 30,000

$= \frac{30,0,00}{20,000} = 1.50$

b. Financial Leverage = EBT = EBIT – Interest

= 20,000-4,000 (50,000x8%)

= 16,000

= 16,000

= 20,000 = 1.25

23. Income statement of Julius Ltd is given below:

Sales	10,50,000	Tax	29,400
Variable cost	7,67,000	Net Income	68,600
Fixed Cost	75,000	No. of equity shares	4,000
EBIT	2,08,000	Calculate 1. DOL 2. DFL, 3.DCL, 4. EPS.	
Interest	1,10,000		

Solution :

Statement of Profit

Sales	10,50,000
Less: Variable cost	7,67,000
Contribution	2,83,000
Less: Fixed cost	75,000
EBIT	2,08,000
Less: Interest	1,10,000
EBT	98,000
Less: Tax	29,400
EAT	68,600

(a) $DOL = \frac{Contribution}{EBIT} = \frac{2,83,000}{2,08,000} = 1.36$

(b) $DFL = \frac{EBIT}{EBT} = \frac{2,0,8,000}{98,000} = 2.12$

(c) DCL = DOL x DFL = 1.36 x 2.12 = 2.28

(d) $EPS = \frac{EAT}{Shares} = \frac{68,600}{4,000} = 17.15$

24. Following informations are taken from the books of a company.

Selling Price	Rs.28 per unit
Variable cost	Rs.18 per unit
Break Even Point	4,000 units

You are required to find out the degree of operating and financial leverages for

(a) 5,000 units of output and

(b) 6,000 units of output.

Note: At Break even point profit is Nil

Solution :

Statement of Profit/Loss at 4,000 Units

Sales (4,000 × 28)	1,12,000
Less: Variable cost (4,000 × 18)	72,000
Contribution	40,000
Less: Fixed cost	40,000
Profit	0

Statement of Profit

	5000 units	6000 units
Sales (28 × 5,000, 28 × 6,000)	1,40,000	1,68,000
Less: Variable cost (18 × 5,000, 18 × 6000)	90,000	1,08,000
Contribution	50,000	60,000
Less: Fixed cost	40,000	40,000
EBIT	10,000	20,000
Less: Interest	-	-
EBT	10,000	20,000
DOL = $\frac{\text{Contribution}}{\text{EBIT}}$	$\frac{50,000}{10,000} = 5$	$\frac{60,000}{20,000} = 3$
DFL = $\frac{\text{EBIT}}{\text{EBT}}$	$\frac{10,000}{10,000} = 1$	$\frac{20,000}{20,000} = 1$

25. A company has sales of Rs.1,00,000. The variable costs are 40% of the sales, while the fixed operating costs amount to Rs.30,000. The amount of interest on long term debt is Rs.10,000.
You are required to calculate the composite leverage and illustrate its impact if sales increase by 5%.

Solution:

Income Statement

Sales	1,00,000
Less: Variable cost (1,00,000x40%)	40,000
Contribution	60,000
Less: Fixed cost	30,000
EBIT	30,000
Less: Interest	10,000
EBT	20,000

$$\text{DOL} = \frac{\text{Contribution}}{\text{EBIT}} = \frac{60,000}{30,000} = 2$$

$$\text{DFL} = \frac{\text{EBIT}}{\text{EBT}} = \frac{30,000}{20,000} = 1.5$$

$$\text{DCL} = \text{DOL} \times \text{DFL} = 2 \times 1.5 = 3$$

If sales increase by 5%

Income Statement

Sales (1,00,000 + 5% of 1,00,000)	1,05,000
Less: Variable cost (1,05,000 × 40%)	42,000
Contribution	63,000
Less: Fixed cost	30,000
EBIT	33,000
Less: Interest	10,000
EBT	23,000

Percentage increase in profits

$$\frac{\text{Increase in per Profits}}{\text{Base Profit}} = \times 100$$

$$\frac{23,000 - 20,000}{20,000} = \times 100 = \times 100 = 15\%$$

26. The following data are available for R and S ltd.

Selling Price	Rs. 120 per unit
Variable Cost	Rs. 70 per unit
Fixed Cost	Rs. 2,00,000

1. What is operating leverage when R and S Ltd., produces and sells 6,000 units.
2. What is the percentage change that will occur in the EBIT, if the output increases by 5%.
3. Calculate revised operating leverage.

Solution :

Statement of Profit

	6000 units	6300 units (6000 + 5%)
Sales (6,000 × 120, 6300 × 120)	7,20,000	7,56,000
Less: Variable cost (6,000 × 70, 6300 × 70)	4,20,000	4,41,000
Contribution	3,00,000	3,15,000
Less: Fixed cost	2,00,000	2,00,000
EBIT	1,00,000	1,15,000

1. Operating leverage at 6,000 units $\frac{\text{Contribution}}{\text{EBIT}}$

$$= \frac{3,00,000}{1,00,000} = 3$$

2. Percentage change in EBIT if the output increase by 5%
   EBIT at 6,300 units = 1,15,000
   EBIT at 6,000 units = 1,00,000
   Increase in EBIT = 15,000

   $$\text{Percentage increase in EBIT} = \frac{15,000}{1,00,000} \times 100 = 15\%$$

3. $$\text{Operating leverage at 6,300 units} = \frac{3,15,000}{1,15,000} = 2.74$$

27. A firm has sales of Rs. 10,00,000 variable cost of Rs. 7,00,000 and fixed cost of Rs. 2,00,000 and debt of Rs. 5,00,000 at 10% rate of interest. What are the operating financial and combined leverage? If the firm wants to double its earnings before interest and tax (EBIT) how much of a rise in sales would be needed on a percentage basis?

Solution :

Statement of Profit

Sales	10,00,000
Less: Variable cost	7,00,000
Contribution	3,00,000
Less: Fixed cost	2,00,000
EBIT	1,00,000
Less: Interest (5,00,000 × 10%)	50,000
EBIT	50,000

(a) $$\text{Operating Leverage} = \frac{\text{Contribution}}{\text{EBIT}} = \frac{3,00,000}{1,00,000} = 3$$

(b) $$\text{Financial Leverage} = \frac{\text{EBIT}}{\text{EBI}} = \frac{1,00,000}{50,000} = 2$$

(c) Combined Leverage = DOL × DFL = 3 × 2 = 6

(d) Increase in sales if EBIT is doubled

Statement of Profit

Sales (See Working)	13,33,333
Less: Variable cost (13,33,333 × 70%)	9,33,333
Contribution	4,00,000
Less: Fixed cost	2,00,000
EBIT	2,00,000

Workings :

Percentage of variable cost to sales $\frac{\text{Vairable Cost}}{\text{Sales}} \times 100$

$$\frac{7,00,000}{10,00,000} \times 100 = 70\%$$

Contribution = Sales – Variable cost = 100 – 70 = 30.
Contribution = EBIT + Fixed Cost = 2,00,000 + 2,00,000 = 4,00,000 If contribution is 30, sales = 100

If contribution is Rs. 4,00,000 = 4,00,000 × $\frac{100}{30}$ = 13,33,333

Increase in sales = 13,33,333 – 10,00,000 = 3,33,333

percentage increase in sales = $\frac{3,33,333}{10,00,000}$ × 100 = 33%.

28. Calculate operating and financial leverages under situations A and B from the following particulars:

Installed Capacity	1,000 units
Actual capacity Utilised	800 units
Selling Price per unit	Rs. 20
Variable cost per unit	Rs. 15
Fixed costs situations A	Rs. 1,000
Situation B	Rs. 1,500

Solution :

Capital structure	*Financial Plan I*	*Financial Plan II*
Equity capital	5,000	7,000
Debt (Cost 10%)	5,000	2,000

Statement of Profit

Particulars	*Situation A*	
	Plan I	*Plan II*
Sales (800 × 20)	16,000	16,000
Less: Variable cost (800 × 15)	12,000	12,000

Contd...

Particulars	*Situation A*	
	Plan I	*Plan II*
Contribution	4,000	4,000
Less: Fixed cost	1,000	1,000
EBIT	3,000	3,000
Less: Interest (5,000 × 10%, 2,000 × 10%)	500	200
EBT	2,500	2,800

(a) Operating Leverage = $\dfrac{\text{Contribution}}{\text{EBIT}} = \dfrac{4,000}{3,000} = 1.33, =$ 1.33

(b) Financial Leverage = $\dfrac{\text{EBIT}}{\text{EBT}} = \dfrac{3,000}{2,500} = 1.2, \dfrac{3,000}{2,800} = 1.07$

Statement of Profit

Particulars	*Situation A*	
	Plan I	*Plan II*
Sales (800x20)	16,000	16,000
Less: Variable cost (800x15)	12,000	12,000
Contribution	4,000	4,000
Less: Fixed cost	1,500	1,500
EBIT	2,500	2,300
Less: Interest	500	200
EBT	2,000	2,300

(a) Operating Leverage = $\dfrac{\text{Contribution}}{\text{EBIT}} = \dfrac{4,000}{2,500}$

$= 1.6, \dfrac{4,000}{2,500} = 1.6$

(b) Financial Leverage = $\dfrac{\text{EBIT}}{\text{EBI}} = \dfrac{2,500}{2,000} = 1.25, \dfrac{2,500}{2,300} = 1.09$

29. Calculate operating and financial leverages under situations A and B from the following information. What are the combinations of operating and financial leverage which give the highest and least value?

    Total Assets Rs. 30,000

    Total Assets Turnover ratio 2

Variable cost as a percentage of sales 60%

Fixed costs: Situations A Rs.6,000

Situation B Rs.9,000

Capital Structure:

Capital structure	*Financial Plan I*	*Financial Plan II*
Equity	30,000	30,000
Debt (Cost 10%)	20,000	30,000

Solution :

Calculation of sales

$$\text{Assets Turnover ratio} = \frac{\text{Sales}}{\text{Total Assets}} = 2:1$$

If total Assets are 1, sales = 2

If total assets are Rs. 30,000, sales = 30,000 × 2/1 = 60,000.

Statement of Profit

Particulars	*Situation A*	
	Plan I	*Plan II*
Sales	60,000	60,000
Less: Variable cost (60% of sales)	36,000	36,000
Contribution	24,000	24,000
Less: Fixed cost	6,000	6,000
EBIT	18,000	18,000
Less: Interest (20,000 × 10%, 30,000 × 10%)	2,000	3,000
EBT	16,000	15,000

(a) $\text{Operating Leverage} = \frac{\text{Contribution}}{\text{EBIT}} = \frac{24,000}{18,000} = 1.33,$

$\frac{24,000}{18,000} = 1.33$

(b) $\text{Financial Leverage} = \frac{\text{EBIT}}{\text{EBT}} = \frac{18,000}{16,000} = 1.125, \frac{18,000}{15,000}$

= 1.2

(c) Combined leverage :

DOL × DFL = 1.33 × 1.125 = 1.496, 1.33 × 1.2 = 1.596

Statement of Profit

Particulars	*Situation A*	
	Plan I	*Plan II*
Sales	60,000	60,000
Less: Variable cost (60% of sales)	36,000	36,000
Contribution	24,000	24,000
Less: Fixed cost	9,000	9,000
EBIT	15,000	15,000
Less: Interest	2,000	3,000
EBT	13,000	12,000

(a) Operating Leverage = $\frac{\text{Contribution}}{\text{EBIT}} = \frac{24,000}{15,000} = 1.4$

$= \frac{24,000}{15,000} = 1.4$

(b) Financial Leverage = $\frac{\text{EBIT}}{\text{EBT}} = \frac{15,000}{13,000} = 1.154, \frac{15,000}{12,000}$

$= 1.25$

(c) Combined leverage :

DOL × DFL = 1.4 × 1.154 = 1.616, 1.4 × 1.25 = 1.75

Highest and least value of combined lever age :

Highest value = 1.75 situation B plan II

Least value = 1.49 situation A plan II

30. The following informations are available in respect of companies M and N.

	Company M	*Company N*
Equity share capital (Rs.10 each)	Rs. 20,00,000	10,00,000
14% Debentures	Rs. 5,00,000	Rs. 15,00,000
EBIT	Rs. 5,00,000	Rs. 5,00,000
Return on capital employed	20%	20%
Tax rate	40%	40%

From the above information, calculate

(a) Financial leverage,

(b) Rate of return on equity share capital,

(c) Earnings per share

Solution :

Statement of Profit

	Company M	*Company N*
EBIT	5,00,000	5,00,000
Less: Interest (14% of EBIT)	70,000	2,10,000
EBT	4,30,000	2,90,000
Less: Tax (40% of EBT)	1,72,000	1,16,000
EAT	2,58,000	1,74,000

Also state which company's share holders are in a better position financially.

(a) Financial Leverage $= \frac{\text{EBIT}}{\text{EBT}} = \frac{5,00,000}{4,30,000} = 1.16, \frac{5,00,000}{2,90,000}$

$= 1.72$

(b) Return equity share capital $= \frac{\text{EAT}}{\text{E.S.Capital}} \times 100$

$= \frac{2,58,000}{20,00,000} \times 100 = 12.9\%, \frac{1,74,000}{10,00,000} \times 100 = 17.4\%$

(c) Earning per share:

$\text{EPS} = \frac{\text{EAT}}{\text{No.of E.Shares}}, \frac{2,58,000}{2,00,000} = 1.29,$

$\frac{1,74,000}{1,00,000} = 1.74$

Comment: The share holders of company N are in a better position financially because their EPS are higher than that of company M. The rate of return on equity share capital in the case of company N is 17.4% as against 12.9% in the case of company M. This is because the company N is getting the benefit of a higher financial leverage.

31. The operating profit of ABC Ltd., is Rs.1,60,000. Its capital structure consists of the following:

10% Debentures	Rs.5,00,000
12% Preference shares	Rs.1,00,000
Equity shares of Rs.100 each	Rs.4,00,000

The company is in 30% tax bracket. Calculate,

(a) Earnings per share (EPS)

(b) Determine the percentage change in EPS associated with 30% increase and 30% decrease in EBIT

(c) The degree of financial leverage

(d) Assuming Dol. 2, determine DCL.

Solution :

(a) Computation of EPS

Particulars	*Present Position Rs.*	*30% increase Rs.*	*30% decrease Rs.*
EBIT	1,60,000	2,08,000	1,12,000
Less: Interest	50,000	50,000	50,000
EBT	1,10,000	1,58,000	62,000
Less: Tax (30% of EBT)	33,000	47,400	18,600
EAT	77,000	1,10,600	43,400
Less: Preference Dividend	12,000	12,000	12,000
Earnings for E.S. holders	65,000	98,600	31,400
No. of equity shares (N)	4,000	4,000	4,000

$$EPS = \frac{\text{Earnings E.S. holders}}{N} = \frac{65,000}{4,000} = 16.25, \frac{98,600}{4,000}$$

$$= 24.65, \frac{31,400}{4,000} = 7.85$$

(b) Percentage in increase in EPS due to 30% increase in EBIT Increase in EPS = 24.65 – 16.25 = – 8.40 Percentage

$$\text{increase in EPS} = \frac{8.40}{16.25} \times 100 = 51.69\%$$

(c) Percentage decrease in EPS due to 30% decrease in EBIT: Decrease in EPS = 16.25 – 7.85 = 8.40 Percentage

$$\text{decrease in EPS} = \frac{8.40}{16.25} \times 100 = 51.69\%$$

(d) Degree of financial leverage = $\frac{\text{EBIT}}{\text{EBT}}$ $\frac{1,60,000}{1,10,000}$ = 1.45,

$\frac{2,08,000}{1,58,00}$ = 1.32, $\frac{1,12,000}{62,000}$ = 1.81

(e) Degree of combined leverage = DOL × DFL = 2 × 1.45 = 2.90, 2 × 1.32 = 2.64, 2 × 1.81 = 3.62

32. A firm has sales of Rs.75,00,000 variable cost of Rs.30,00,000 and fixed cost of Rs.9,00,000. It has a debt of Rs.40,00,000 at 10% and equity of Rs.50,00,000.
    (a) What is the firms return of investment (ROI)?
    (b) Does it have favourable financial leverage?
    (c) If a firms belongs to an industry whose assets turnover is 2, does if have a high or low asset leverage?

Solution :

Statement of Profit

Sales	75,00,000
Less: Variable cost	30,00,000
Contribution	45,00,000
Less: Fixed cost	9,00,000
EBIT	36,00,000
Less: Interest (40,00,000 × 10%)	4,00,000
EBT	32,00,000

(d) What is the operating leverage if the firm?

(e) If the sales drop of Rs.50,00,000 what will

(a) Return on Investment (ROI) = $\frac{\text{EBIT}}{\text{Captial Employed}} \times 100$

Capital Employed = Debt + Equity

= 40,00,000 + 50,00,000

= 90,00,000

$= \frac{36,00,000}{90,00,000} \times 100 = 40\%$

(b) Financial leverage = $\frac{\text{EBIT}}{\text{EBT}} = \frac{36,00,000}{32,00,000} = 1.125$

The firm's ROI (40%) is much higher than the cost of debt 10%. Hence it has a favourable financial leverage.

(c) Assets Turnover = $\frac{\text{Net Sales}}{\text{Total Assets}}$

Total Liabilities = Total Assets

Debt Equity = Total Assets

$40{,}00{,}000 + 50{,}00{,}000 = 90{,}00{,}000 = \frac{75{,}00{,}000}{90{,}00{,}000} = 0.83$

The firm assets turnover is 0.83 which is much lower than that of an industry assets turnover of 2 times. Hence, it has a low assets leverage.

(d) Operating Leverage = $\frac{\text{Contribution}}{\text{EBIT}} = \frac{45{,}00{,}000}{36{,}00{,}000} = 1.25.$

(e) Calculation of new EBIT when sales drop to Rs. 50,00,000:

Sales	50,00,000
Less: Variable cost 40% (See working)	20,00,000
Contribution	30,00,000
Less: Fixed cost	9,00,000
EBIT	21,00,000

Percentage of variable cost = $\frac{30{,}00{,}000}{75{,}00{,}000} \times 100 = 40\%$

33. 1. Find the operating leverage from the following data: Sales Rs.50,000, variable cost 60% fixed cost Rs.12,000

2. Find the financial leverage from the following data:
Net worth Rs.25,00,000, Debt / Equity 3/1
Interest rate 12%
Operating profit Rs.20,00,000

Solution :

Computation of Operating Profit

Sales	50,000
Less: Variable cost (60% of sales)	30,000
Contribution	20,000
Less: Fixed cost	12,000
EBIT	8,000

1. Operating leverage = $\frac{\text{Contribution}}{\text{EBIT}} = \frac{20,000}{8,000} = 2.5$

2. Financial Leverage = $\frac{\text{EBIT}}{\text{EBIT}}$

EBIT = 20,00,000

Less: Interest (75,00,000 × 12%) = 9,00,000

EBT

= 11,00,000

$$\text{DFL} = \frac{20,00,000}{11,00,000} = 1.82.$$

Debt/ Equity = 3/1 ie = 3 : 1

Equity refers to net worth = Rs.25,00,000 = $\frac{\text{Debt}}{25,00,000}$ 3:1

$$\therefore \text{ Debt} = 25,00,000 \times 3 = 75,00,000 = \frac{20,00,000}{11,00,000} = 1.82$$

34. The following information are available regarding Biral Cement Ltd.

Profit before depreciation, Interest and tax	82,50,000
Depreciation	15,00,000
Tax Rate	30%
Earnings per share	4.20
No. of equity shares	3,00,000

Solution :

Calculate Degree of Financial Leverage

Profit before depreciation, Interest and Tax	82,50,000
Depreciation	15,00,000
Profit before interest and Tax (EBIT)	67,50,000

$$\text{EPS} = \frac{\text{EBIT}}{\text{No. of Equity shares}} = 4.20$$

$$= \frac{\text{EBIT}}{3,00,000} = 4.20$$

EBIT = 3,00,000 × 4.20 = 12,60,000
Tax rate = 30%
Profit before Tax = 100
Less: Tax EBT = 30
EAT = 70
EAT is 70, EBT = 100
EAT is 12,60,000, EBT = 12,60,000 × 100/70 = 18,00,000

Tax = EBT – EAT = 18,00,000 – 12,60,000 = 5,40,000

Interest = EBIT – EBT

= 67,50,000-18,00,000 = 49,50,000

EBIT = 67,50,000
Less: Interest = 49,50,000
EBT = 18,00,000
Less: Tax = 5,40,000
EAT = 12,60,000

$$DFL = \frac{EBIT}{EBIT} = \frac{67,50,000}{18,00,000} = 3.75$$

35. The following estimates are made for wheels India Ltd for the year 2005-2006.

(a) The degree of operating leverage is expected to be 1.5,

(b) Fixed costs are estimated to be Rs. 2.5 lakhs.

(c) Interest on Rs. 30 lakhs debt will be paid at 10%

Solution :

You are required to calculate the degree of financial leverage and degree of total leverage.

$$DOL = \frac{Contribution}{EBIT} = 1.5 \quad \frac{Contribution}{contribution - Fixed\,Cost} = 1.5$$

1.5 (Contribution – Fixed cost) = Contribution

1.5 (Contribution = 2,50,000) = Contribution

1.5 Contribution = 3,75,000 = Contribution

1.5 Contribution - 1 Contribution = 3,75,000

0.5 Contribution = 3,75,000

$$\text{Contribution } \frac{3,75,000}{0.5} = 7,50,000$$

EBIT = Contribution – Fixed cost

= 7,50,000 – 2,50,000 = 5,00,000

EBT = EBIT - Interest

= 5,00,000 – (30,00,000 × 10/100)

5,00,000 – 3,00,000 = 2,00,000

$$\text{(a) DFL} = \frac{\text{EBIT}}{\text{EBIT}} = \frac{5,00,000}{2,00,000} = 2.5$$

(b) Degree of Total leverage = DOL × DFL

= 1.5 × 2.5 = 3.75

36. From the following, prepare in come statement for company x and y.

	Company X	*Company Y*
Financial Leverage	3:1	4:1
Interest	Rs.200	Rs.600
Operating Leverage	4:1	5:1
Variable cost as a % of sales	75%	50%
Income tax	45%	45%

Solution :

Income Statement

Particulars	Company X (Rs)	Company Y (Rs)
Sales (100%)	4,800	8,000
Less: Variable cost(75%, 50%)	3,600	4,000
Contribution (Workings 25%, 50%)	1,200	4,000
Less: Fixed Cost	900	3,200
EBIT (Working)	300	800
Less: Interest (Working)	200	600
EBT (Working)	100	200
Less: Tax 45%	45	90
EAT	55	110

Workings

Company X

$$\text{(a) Financial leverage} = \frac{\text{EBIT}}{\text{EBIT}} = 3:1$$

EBIT – EBT = Interest

3 - 1 = 2

If interest is 2, EBT = 1

If interest is Rs.200, EBT = ?

200 × 1/2 = Rs.100

EBIT = EBT + Interest = 100+200 = Rs.300

(b) Operating Leverage = $\frac{\text{Contribution}}{\text{EBIT}}$ = 4:1

If EBIT is 1, contribution = 4

If EBIT is Rs.300, contribution = ?

Contribution = 300 × 4	= 1,200
Contribution	= 1,200
Less: Fixed cost	= 900
EBIT	= 300

Company Y:

(a) Financial Leverage = $\frac{\text{EBIT}}{\text{EBIT}}$ = 4:1

EBIT – EBT = Interest

4 - 1 = 3

If interest is 3, EBT = 1

If Interest is 600, EBT = ?

EBT = 600 × 1/3 = 200

EBIT = EBT + Interest = 200 + 600 = 800

(b) Operating Leverage = = 5:1

If EBIT is 1, contribution = 5

If EBIT is 800, contribution = ?

Contribution = 800 × 5 = 4,000

Contribution	= 4,000
Less: Fixed cost	= 3,200
EBIT	= 800

37. If the combined leverage and operating leverage of a company are 2.5 and 1.25 respectively, find the financial

leverage and P.V. ratio, given that the equity dividend per share is Rs.2, interest payable per year is Rs.1,00,000, total fixed cost Rs.50,000 and sales Rs.10,00,000.

Combined leverage = 2.5
Operating Leverage = 1.25
Financial Leverage = ?

Combined Leverage = Operating Leverage x Financial Leverage

$$2.5 = 1.25 \times ?$$

or

Operating Leverage = financial Leverage x combined leverage

Solution :

$$\text{Financial Leverage} = \frac{\text{Combined Laverage}}{\text{Operating Leverage}} = \frac{2.5}{1.25} = 2$$

$$\text{Financial Leverage} = \frac{\text{EBIT}}{\text{EBT}} = 2:1$$

EBIT – Interest = EBT
2 - 1 = 1

If interest is 1, EBIT = 2

If interest is 1,00,000, EBIT = ?

EBIT = 1,00,000 × 2 = 2,00,000

EBT = EBIT – Interest

= 2,00,000 – 1,00,000 = 1,00,000

$$\text{Operating Leverage} = \frac{\text{Contribution}}{\text{EBIT}} = 1.25:1$$

If EBIT is 1, Contribution = 1.25

If EBIT is 2,00,000, Contribution = ?

Contribution = 2,00,000 × 1.25 = 2,50,000

$$\text{Profit volume ratio (PVR)} = \frac{\text{Contribution}}{\text{Sales}} \times 100 = \frac{2{,}50{,}000}{10{,}00{,}000} \times 100 = 25\%$$

38. Birla Steel Ltd has a financial leverage of 4 and operating of 5. The interest payment on borrowings during the year was Rs.3,00,000. The variable cost is 75% of sales. Tax rate is 30%. You are required to prepare income statement of Birla Steel Ltd for the year 2005.

Solution :

(a) $\text{DFL} = \dfrac{\text{EBIT}}{\text{EBIT} - \text{Interest}} = 4$

$4(\text{EBIT} - \text{Interest}) = \text{EBIT}$

$4\ \text{EBIT} - (4 \times 3{,}00{,}000) = \text{EBIT}$

$4\ \text{EBIT} - 12{,}00{,}000 = \text{EBIT}$

$4\text{EBIT} - \text{EBIT} = 12{,}00{,}000$

$3\ \text{EBIT} = 12{,}00{,}000$

$\text{EBIT} = \dfrac{12{,}00{,}000}{3} = 4{,}00{,}000$

(b) $\text{DOL} = \dfrac{\text{Contribution}}{\text{EBIT}} = 5$

5 × EBIT = Contribution

5 × 4,00,000 = Contribution

Contribution = 20,00,000

Contribution = Sales – Variable cost

Variable cost is 75% of sales

Contribution = 100-75 = 25

If contribution is 25, sales = 100

If contribution is 20,00,000, sales = ?

Sales = 20,00,000 × 100/25 = 80,00,000

Sales = 80,00,000

Variable = 80,00,000 × 75/100 = 60,00,000

Fixed cost = Contribution – EBIT

= 20,00,000 – 4,00,000

= 16,00,000

Income Statement

Sales	80,00,000
Less: Variable cost	60,00,000
Contribution	20,00,000
Less: Fixed cost	16,00,000
EBIT	4,00,000
Less: Interest	3,00,000
EBT	1,00,000
Less: Tax 30%	30,000
EAT	70,000

CHAPTER 4

CAPITAL STRUCTURE

DEFINITION

Capital structure is the permanent financing of the firm represented by long term debt, preference share and network- Western & Brighten.

FACTORS AFFECTING THE CAPITAL STRUCTURE

1. Trading on equity
2. Desire to control of business
3. Nature of the business
4. Purpose of financing
5. Period of financing

OBJECTIVES OF SOUND WORKING CAPITAL STRUCTURE

1. Economic objectives
   - i. Minimization of cost
   - ii. Minimisation of risk
   - iii. Maximisation of return
   - iv. Persuation of control
   - v. Property liquidity
   - vi. Full utilization
2. Other objectives
   - i. Simplicity
   - ii. Flexibility

NECESSITY OF CHANGES IN CAPITAL STRUCTURE

1. To restore balance by reducing the fixed charge on finance.
2. To simplify the structure by consolidating various securities.
3. To attract investors
4. To capitalize its retained earnings
5. To meet certain legal requirements
6. To fund accumulated dividend
7. Borrowing at higher rate
8. Purchase of assets in boom period
9. Insufficient provision for depreciation
10. High rate of taxation
11. low production.

UNDER CAPITALISATION

Meanings

Real value of the company is much more higher than is reflected by back value. It is just the opposite to over capitalization.

Causes

1. Under estimation of capital requirement
2. Under estimation of future earnings
3. Secret reserves.
4. Difficulty in procurement of capital
5. Maintaining the high efficiently

MEASURES TO CORRECT UNDER CAPITALIZATION

1. Increase the par value of shares
2. Issue of bonus shares
3. Fresh issue of shares

MEANING OF CAPITAL STRUCTURE

Capital structure refers to the make up of the capitalistion capital structure divide the capital into capital of the owners and outsiders So the capital structure means an ideal combination of owned fund and borrowed funds.

Forms of Capital Structure

1. Equity shares

   Equity share capital is raised from share holders and there is only one share capital called equity share capital.
2. Equity and preference shares

   Capital structure is a mixture of equity and preference shares.
3. Equity preference share and debenture
4. Compound interest

   Accumulated investment interest is known as compound interest.

Definition of Compound Interest

Interest is calculated upon the original sum invested or lend plus accumulated interest is called compound interest.

Formula

$A = P(1 + r)^n$

A = Compound interest

P = Principle amount

R = Rate of interest

N = Number of years

Time Value of Money

Money has time value A rupee to day is more valuable than a rupee after a year because money value is increased and decreased over a period.

Several Reason for Time Value of Money

1. Increased future consumption
2. Money value is inflated
3. Individual in general prefer current consumption rather than future consumption.

Basic Theory

1. Net Income (NI) Approach
2. Net Operating Income (NOI) Approach
3. Modigliani and Miller (MM) approach
4. Traditional Approach

Patterns of Capital Structure

In case of new company the capital structure may be of any of the following four patterns,

1. Capital structures with equity shares only
2. Capital structure with equity and preference shares
3. Capital structure with equity shares and debentures
4. Capital structure with equity shares, preference shares and debentures.

Capital Structure Theories

There are four major theories/approaches explaining the relationship between capital structure, cost of capital and value of the firm.

1. Net Income (NI) Approach
2. Net Operating Income (NOI) Approach
3. Modifilant–Miller (MM) Approach and
4. Traditional Approach

1. *Net Income (NI) Approach:* This approach has been suggested by Durand. According to this approach. Capital structure decisions is relevant to the valuation of the firm. In other words, a change in the capital structure causes a corresponding change in the overall cost of capital as well as the total value of the firm.

   Net Income approach is based on the following three assumptions.

   i. There are no corporate taxes

ii. The cost of debt is less than cost of equity capitalization rate.

iii. The debt content does not change the risk perception of the investors.

The value of the firm on the basis of NI Approach can be ascertained as follows.

$$V = S + B$$

Where V = Value of Firm

S = Market Value of Equity

B = Market Value of Debt

Market value of equity can be ascertained as follows.

S =

Where S = Market Value of Equity

NI = Earnings available for equity shareholders

Ke = Equity capitalization rate

2. *Net Operating Income (NOI) Approach:* This approach has also been suggested by Durand. This is just opposite of Net Income Approach. According to this approach the market value of the firm is not at all affected by the capital structure changes. The market value of the firm is ascertained by capitalizing the net operating income at the overall cost of capital (K). Which is considered to be constant. The market value of equity is ascertained by deducting the market value of the debt from the market value of the firm.

Assumptions

The Net Operating Income (NOI) approach is based on the following assumptions.

1. The overall cost of capital (K) remains constant for all degrees of debt equity mix or leverage.
2. The market capitalizes the value of the firm as a whole and therefore, the split between debt and equity is not relevant.

3. The use of debt having low cost increases the risk of equity shareholders.
4. There are no corporate taxes.

Value of the Firm

According to the NOI approach the value of a firm can be determined by the following equation.

$$V = \frac{EBIT}{K}$$

Where V = Value of the firm

K = Overall cost of capital

EBIT = Earnings before Interest and Tax

Value of Equity

$$S = V - B$$

Where,

S = Value of Equity

V = Value of Firm

B = Value of debt

3. *Modigiliant – Miller (MM) Approach:* The MM approach is similar to the NOI approach. In other words according to this approach, the value of a firm is independent of its capital structure. However there is a basic difference between the two. The NOI approach is purely definitional or conceptual. It does not provide operational justification for relevance of the capital structure in the valuation of the firm.

Assumptions

The MM approach is subject to the following assumptions.

1. Capital Markets are perfect, this means
   a. Investors are free to buy and sell securities
   b. The investors can borrow without restriction on the same terms on which the firm can borrow.

c. Investors are well informed
d. The investors behave rationally and
e. There are no transaction costs

2. The firms can be classified into homogeneous risk classes
3. All investors have the same expectation of firm's net operating income (EBIT) with which to evaluate the value of any firm.
4. The dividend pay out ratio is 100% in other words, there are no retained earnings.
5. There are no corporate taxes, However this assumption has been removed later.

Limitations of MM Hypothesis

1. Rates of interest are not the same for the individuals and the firms.
2. Home made leverage is not perfect substitute for corporate leverage.
3. Transaction costs involved.
4. Institutional Restrictions
5. Corporate taxes frustrate MM hypothesis

4. *Traditional Approach:* In the proceeding discussion we have explained that the NI approach and NOI approach represent two extremes. According to NI approach, the debt content in the capital structure affects both the overall cost, capital and total valuation of the firm while NOI approach suggests that capital structure is totally irrelevant so far as total valuation of the firm is concerned.
   1. The traditional approach is similar to NI approach to the extent.
   2. It subscribes to the NOI approach that beyond and certain degree of leverages the overall cost of capital increased resulting in decrease in the total value of the firm.

Features of an Approach to Capital Structure

1. Profitability
2. Solvency
3. Flexibility
4. Conservation
5. Control

Net Income Approach (NI)

Particulars	Amount
EBIT	xxx
Less: Interest ($I = B \times Ki$)	xxx
EBT	xxx
Equity Capitalization rate (Ke)	xxx
Market Value of Equity $\left(S = \frac{EBT}{Ke}\right)$	xxx
Market value of debt $\left(B = \frac{I}{Ki}\right)$	xxx
Total market value of the firm ($S + B = v$)	xxx

Overall cost of capital

$$K_0 = \frac{EBIT}{V} \times 100$$

Alternatively

$$K_0 = \left(Ki \times \frac{B}{V}\right) + \left(Ke \times \frac{S}{V}\right)$$

Practical Problems

Basic Theory

1. Net Income (NI) Approach
2. Net Operating Income (NOI) Approach
3. Traditional Approach
4. Modigliani–Miller (MM) Approach

I. Net Income (NI) Approach

Particulars	Rs.
Earnings Before Interest and Taxes (EBIT)	xxx
Less : Interest (I = B × Ki)	xxx
Earnings Before Tax (EBT)	xxx
Equity Capitalisation Rate (Ke)	xxx
Market value of Equity (S = EBT/Ke)	xxx
Market value of Debt (B = I/Ki)	xxx
Total Market value of the firm (r = S + B)	xxx

Overall cost of capital (or) weighted average cost of capital (Ko)

$$Ko = \frac{EBIT}{V} \times 100$$

Alternatively

$$Ko = \left[Ki \times \frac{B}{V}\right] + \left[Ke \times \frac{S}{V}\right]$$

1. A company with net operating earnings of Rs.3,00,000 is attempting to evaluate a number of possible capital structures, given below which of the capital structure will you recommend and why ?

Capital Structure	*Debt in Capital Structure (Rs.)*	*Cost of Debt Ki(%)*	*Cost of Equity Ke (%)*
1	3,00,000	10	12.0
2	4,00,000	10	12.5
3	5,00,000	11	13.5
4	6,00,000	12	15.0
5	7,00,000	14	18.0

Solution :

Determination of Overall Cost of Capital

Particulars	*I*	*II*	*III*	*IV*	*V*
EBIT	3,00,000	3,00,000	3,00,000	3,00,000	3,00,000
Less : Interest	30,000	40,000	55,000	72,000	98,000
EBT	2,70,000	2,60,000	2,45,000	2,28,000	2,02,000

Contd...

Particulars	*I*	*II*	*III*	*IV*	*V*
Equity Capitalisation rate (Ke)	0.12	0.125	0.135	0.150	0.180
Market value Equity S = $\frac{EBT}{Ke}$	22,50,000	20,80,000	18,14,815	15,20,000	11,22,222
Market value of Debt (B)	3,00,000	4,00,000	5,00,000	6,00,000	7,00,000
Total Market value (V = S + B)	25,50,000	24,80,000	23,14,815	21,20,000	18,22,222
Overall cost of captal (Ko = EBIT/V × 100)	11.76%	12.10%	12.95%	14.155%	16.46%

Capital structure having debt of Rs.3,00,000 recommend.

2. Assuming no taxes and given the earnings before interest and taxes (EBIT), interest (I) at 10% and equity capitalization rate (ke) below, calculate the total market value of each firm.

Firms	*EBIT Rs.*	*I Rs.*	*Ke*
A	2,00,000	20,000	12%
B	3,00,000	60,000	16%
C	5,00,000	2,00,000	15%
D	6,00,000	2,40,000	18%

Also determine the weighted average cost of capital for each firm.

Solution :

Determination of Overall Cost of Capital

Particulars	*A*	*B*	*C*	*D*
EBIT	2,00,000	3,00,000	5,00,000	6,00,000
Less : Interest	20,000	60,000	2,00,000	2,40,000
EBT	1,80,000	2,40,000	3,00,000	3,60,000
Equity Capitalization (Ke) Rate	0.12	0.16	0.15	0.18

Contd...

Particulars	*A*	*B*	*C*	*D*
Market value of Equity $S = \frac{EBT}{Ke}$	15,00,000	15,00,000	20,00,000	20,00,000
Market value of Debt (B) = I/0.10	2,00,000	6,00,000	20,00,000	24,00,000
Total Market value (V = S + B)	17,00,000	21,00,000	40,00,000	44,00,000
Overall cost of captal (Ko = EBIT/V × 100)	11.76%	14.29%	12.5%	13.64%

Capital structure having debt of Rs. 2,00,000 is recommend.

3. A Company wishes to determine the optimum capital structure from the following information.

Situation	*Debt Rs.*	*Equity Rs.*	*Kd*	*Ke*
1	4,00,000	1,00,000	9%	10%
2	2,50,000	2,50,000	6%	11%
3	1,00,000	4,00,000	5%	14%

Which is the optimal capital structure.

Solution :

Determination of Overall Cost of Capital

Particulars	*1*	*2*	*3*
EBIT	46,000	12,500	51,000
Less : Interest	36,000	15,000	5,000
EBT	10,000	27,500	56,000
Equity Capitalization Rate (Ke)	0.10	0.11	0.14
Market value of Equity $S = \frac{EBT}{Ke}$	1,00,000	2,50,000	4,00,000
Market value of Debt (B)	4,00,000	2,50,000	1,00,000
Total Market value (V = S + B)	5,00,000	5,00,000	5,00,000
Overall cost of captal (Ko = EBIT/V × 100)	9.20%	2.50%	10.20%

Capital structure having debt of Rs. 2,50,000 is recommend.

4. A company expects a net income of Rs. 80,000. It has Rs. 2,00,000, 8% debentures. The equity capitalization rate

is 10%. Calculate the value of firm and over all capitalization rate under net income approach.

Solution :

EBIT	80,000
Less : Interest (2,00,000 × 8%)	16,000
EBT	64,000
Equity Capitalization Rate (Ke)	0.10
Market value of Equity (S = EBT /Ke)	6,40,000
Market value of debt (B)	2,00,000
Total market value (V = S + B)	8,40,000
Overall cost of capital (Ko = EBIT/V × 100)	9.52%

5. A company has net income of Rs. 80,000. 1. It has 8% debentures of Rs. 2,00,000. The equity capitalization rate is 10%. Calculate (under NI method) the value of firm and over all capitalization rate. 2. Also calculate them, if the debentures are increased to Rs. 3,00,000 at 6%.

Solution :

Determination of Overall Cost of Capital

Particulars	*1*	*2*
EBIT	80,000	80,000
Less : Interest (2,00,000 × 8%, 3,00,000 × 8%)	16,000	18,000
EBT	64,000	62,000
Equity Capitalization Rate (Ke)	0.10	0.10
Market value of Equity $S = \frac{EBT}{Ke}$	6,40,000	6,20,000
Market value of Debt (B)	2,00,000	3,00,000
Total Market value (V = S + B)	8,40,000	9,20,000
Overall cost of capital (Ko = EBIT/V × 100)	9.52%	8 .70%

Capital structure having debt of Rs. 3,00,000 is recommend.

6. Krishna Ltd is expecting and annual EBIT of Rs. 2,00,000. The company has Rs. 7,00,000 in 10% debentures. The cost of equity capital or capitalization rate is 12.5%. You are required to calculate the total value of the firm. Also ascertain the overall cost of capital?

Solution :

Computation of Overall Cost of Capital

Particulars	*Rs.*
EBIT	2,00,000
Less : Interest (7,00,000 × 10%)	70,000
EBT	1,30,000
Equity Capitalization Rate (Ke)	0.125
Market value of Equity S = $\frac{\text{EBT}}{\text{Ke}}$	10,40,000
Market value of Debt (B)	7,00,000
Total Market value (V = S + B)	17,40,000
Overall cost of capital (Ko = EBIT/V × 100)	7.47%

7. Bharathi Ltd. expects an annual EBIT of Rs. 1,00,000. The company as Rs. 4,00,000 in debentures. The equity capitalization rate is 12.5%. The company proposes to issue additional equity shares of Rs.1,00,000 and use the proceeds for redemption of debentures of Rs. 1,00,000. Calculate the value of the firm (V) and the overall cost of capital (Ko).

Solution :

Determination of Overall Cost of Capital

Particulars	*Rs.*
EBIT	1,00,000
Less : Interest (4,00,000–1,00,000 = 3,00,000 × 10%)	30,000
EBT	70,000
Equity Capitalization Rate (Ke)	0.125
Market value of Equity S =	5,60,000
Market value of Debt (B)	3,00,000
Total Market value (V = S + B)	8,60,000
Overall cost of capital (Ko = EBIT/V × 100)	11.63%

8. a. A company expects a net operating income of Rs.1,00,000. The equity capitalization rate of the company is 10%. It has Rs.5,00,000 6% debentures. Calculate the value of the firm and overall capitalization rate according to the net income approach (ignore income tax).

b. If the firm's debentures are increased to Rs.7,00,000 what shall be the value of firm and overall capitalization rate ?

Solution :

a. Determination of overall cost of capital

Particulars	*Rs.*
EBIT	1,00,000
Less : Interest (5,00,000 × 6%)	30,000
EBT	70,000
Equity Capitalization Rate (Ke)	0.10
Market value of Equity S = $\frac{EBT}{Ke}$	7,00,000
Market value of Debt (B)	5,00,000
Total Market value (V = S + B)	12,00,000
Overall cost of capital (Ko = EBIT/V × 100)	8.33%

b. Value of the firm if debentures are increased to Rs. 7,00,000

EBIT	1,00,000
Less : Interest (7,00,000 × 6%)	42,000
EBT	58,000
Equity Capitalization Rate (Ke)	0.10
Market value of Equity S = $\frac{EBT}{Ke}$	5,80,000
Market value of Debt (B)	7,00,000
Total Market value (V = S + B)	12,80,000
Overall cost of capital (Ko = EBIT/V × 100)	7.81

9. X ltd is expecting an annual EBIT of Rs. 1,00,000. The company has Rs. 4,00,000 in 10% debentures. The equity capitalization rate is 12.5%. The company decide to raise Rs. 1,00,000 by issue of 10% debentures, and use the proceeds there of redeem equity shares.
You are require to calculate the total value of the firm and also the overall cost of capital.

Solution :

Particulars	*Rs.*
EBIT	1,00,000
Less : Interest(4,00,000 +1,00,000 x 10%)	50,000
EBT	50,000
Equity Capitalization Rate (Ke)	0.125
Market value of Equity $S = \frac{EBT}{Ke}$	4,00,000
Market value of Debt (B)	5,00,000
Total Market value (V = S + B)	9,00,000
Overall cost of capital (Ko = EBIT/V × 100)	11.1%

II. Net Operating Income (NOI) Approach

10. Blue sky Ltd has an EBIT Rs.2,00,000. The cost of debt is 10% and the outstanding debt is Rs.9,00,000. The overall capitalization (Ko) is 12.5%.

    Calculate the total value of the firm (V) and equity capitalization rate (Ke).

Solution :

Determination of Equity Capitalisation Rate

Particulars	*Rs.*
EBIT	2,00,000
Less : Interest	90,000
EBT	1,10,000
Equity Capitalization Rate (Ko)	0.125
Total Market value V =	16,00,000
Less : Market value of Debt (B)	9,00,000
Market value of Equity (S)	7,00,000
Equity Capitalisation Rate (Ke = EBT/S × 100)	15.71%

11. a. A Ltd expects a net operating income of Rs. 1,20,000. It has Rs. 6,00,000, 6% debentures. The overall capitalization rate is 10%. Calculate the value of the firm and cost of equity according to the net operating income (NOI) approach.

    b. What will be the value of the firm and cost of equity if debentures debt is increased to Rs. 9,00,000.

Solution :

a. Determination of Equity capitalisation rate

Particulars	*Rs.*
EBIT	1,20,000
Less : Interest 6,00,000 × 6%	36,000
EBT	84,000
Overall Capitalization Rate (Ko)	0.10
Total Market value (V = EBIT/Ko)	12,00,000
Less : Market Value of Debt (B)	6,00,000
Market value of Equity (S)	6,00,000
Equity Capitalisation rate (Ke = EBT /S × 100)	14%

b. If debenture is increased to Rs. 9,00,000.

Particulars	*Rs.*
EBIT	1,20,000
Less : Interest 9,00,000 × 6%	54,000
EBT	66,000
Overall Capitalization Rate (Ko)	0.10
Total Market value (V = S + B, V = EBIT/Ko)	12,00,000
Less : Market Value of Debt (B)	9,00,000
Market value of Equity (S)	3,00,000
Equity Capitalisation rate (Ke = EBT /S × 100)	22%

When the proportion of debt had increased, cost of equity had also increased from 14% to 22%. But the overall cost of capital and value of the firm remain unchanged.

12. A company expects a net operating income of Rs.1,00,000. It has Rs.5,00,000 6% debentures. The overall capitalization rate is 10%. Calculate the value of the firm and the equity capitalization rate (cost of equity) according to the net operating income approach.

Solution :

Determination of Equity Capitalization Rate

Particulars	*Rs.*
EBIT	1,00,000
Less : Interest 6,00,000 × 6%	30,000
EBT	70,000

Contd...

Particulars	*Rs.*
Overall Capitalization Rate (Ko)	0.10
Total Market value (V = S + B, V = EBIT/Ko))	10,00,000
Less : Market Value of Debt (B)	5,00,000
Market value of Equity (S)	5,00,000
Equity Capitalisation rate (Ke = EBT /S × 100)	14%

III. Traditional Approach

13. Compute the market value of the firm, market value of equity and the average cost of capital.

	Rs.
Net operating Income	3,00,000
Total Investment	15,00,000
Equity capitalization rate	

a. If the firm uses no debt 10%

b. If the firm uses adebt of Rs.6,00,000 11%

c. The dept of uses Rs.6,00,000 can be raised at 5% rate of interest while debt of Rs.9,00,000 can be raised at 7%. If the firm uses a debt of Rs.9,00,000.

Solution :

Market Value of Firm, Value of Equity and Average Cost of Capital

Particulars	*No debt*	*5% debentures*	*7% debentures*
EBIT	3,00,000	3,00,000	3,00,000
Less : Interest	-	30,000	63,000
EBT	3,00,000	2,70,000	2,27,000
Equity capitalization rate (Ke)	0.10	0.11	0.12
Market value of Equity (S) (S = EBT/Ke)	30,00,000	24,54,545	19,75,000
Market value of debt (B)	-	6,00,000	9,00,000
Total Market value (V) (V = S + B)	30,00,000	30,54,545	28,75,000
Overall cost of capital (or) Average cost of capital Ko = EBIT/V x100	10%	9.82%	10.43%

14. Compute the market value of firm, value of share and average cost of capital from the following information.

Net Operating income	Rs. 2,00,000
Total Investment	Rs. 10,00,000

Equity Capitalisation Rate :

1. If the firm uses no debt 10%
2. If the firm uses 5% Rs. 4,00,000 debentures 11%
3. If the firm uses 6% Rs. 6,00,000 debentures 13%

Solution :

Market Value of Firm, Value of Equity and Average Cost of Capital

Particulars	*No debt*	*5% debentures*	*6% debentures*
EBIT	2,00,000	2,00,000	2,00,000
Less: Interest 4,00,000 × 5%, 6,00,000 × 6%	-	20,000	36,000
EBT	2,00,000	1,80,000	1,64,000
Equity capitalization rate (Ke)	0.10	0.11	0.13
Market value of equity (S) (S = EBT/Ke)	20,00,000	16,36,364	12,61,538
Market value of Debt (B)	-	4,00,000	6,00,000
Total market value (V = S + B)	20,00,000	20,36,364	18,61,538
Overall cost of capital Ko = EBIT/V × 100s	10%	9.82%	10.74%

15. A company current earnings before interest and taxes (EBIT) are Rs.4,00,000. The firm currently has out standing Rs. 15,00,000 of debts at an average cost (Ki) of 10%. Its cost of equity capital (Ke) is estimated to equal 16%.
    1. Determine the current value of the firm using the traditional valuation approach.
    2. Determine the firms overall capitalization rate and both types of leverage ratios.

       a. B/S and b. B/V
    3. The firm is considering reducing its leverage by selling Rs.5,00,000 of equity in order to redeem of Rs.5,00,000. The cost of debt is unaffected the equity capitalization rate is 14%.

Solution :

1. Value of the firm (Traditional Approach)

Particulars	*Rs.*
EBIT	4,00,000
Less : Interest (15,00,000 × 10%)	1,50,000
EBT	2,50,000
Equity capitalisation rate (Ke)	0.16
Market value of equity (S = EBT/Ke)	15,62,500
Market value of Debt (B)	15,00,000
Total Market Value (V = S + B)	30,62,500

2. Overall capitalisation rate (Ko = EBIT/V × 100) 13.06%

   a. $B/S = \frac{15,00,000}{15,62,500} = 0.96$

   b. $B/V = \frac{15,00,000}{30,00,500} = 0.49$

3. Determination of overall cost of capital

EBIT	4,00,000
Less: Interest(15,00,000 – 5,00,000= 10,00,000 x 10%)	1,00,000
EBT	3,00,000
Equity capitalisation Rate (Ke)	0.14
Market value of Equity (S = EBT/Ke)	21,42,857
Market value of Debt (B)	10,00,000
Total Market value (V = S +B)	31,42,857

Overall capitalisation rate

$$Ko = \frac{EBIT}{V} \times 100$$

$$= \frac{4,00,000}{31,42,857} \times 100 = 12.72\%$$

16. A company wholly financed through equity, has a current market value of Rs.16,00,000, the equity capitalisation rate (Ke) is 12.5% and expansion program plan that will involve Rs.5,00,000 in capital expenditure in the current year. The financial manager suggests that debt should be

used to finance atleast part of Rs 5,00,000. Assuming tax rate of 50%. Determine weighted average cost of capital and value of the company for each of the following alternatives developed by the financial manager.

Debt Rs. in lakhs	*Equity Rs. in lakhs*	*Cost of debt Ki(%)*	*Cost of equity Ke(%)*	*Overall cost of capital Ko(%)*
-	16	-	12.5	12.5
1.0	-	10.0	12.6	-
2.0	-	10.4	13.0	-
3.0	-	11.0	14.0	-
4.0	-	12.0	15.0	-
5.0	-	13.0	17.0	-

Which financing plan would you recommend any why?

Solution :

Workings

Determining of EBIT

16,00,000 × 12.5/100 = 2,00,000

EBIT = 2,00,000/1-0.50 = Rs. 4,00,000

(See Table, Page 130 : 16th Answer: Computation of Overall Cost of Capital)

IV. Modigliani and Miller Approach or M. M. Approach

17. Two firms L and U are identical in all respects except for the debt equity mix. Firm L has issued 12% debentures of Rs.15,00,000. Firm U has no debt. Both L and U earn 30% before interest and taxes on their total assets of Rs. 20,00,000.

    The tax rate is 50% and equity capitalisation rate is 20%. Compute the value of the two firms using

    1. Net Income Approach
    2. Net Operating Income Approach

Solution :

Computation of value of firms

1. Net Income Approach

16TH ANSWER

Computation of Overall Cost of Capital

EBIT	*Interest*	*EBIT*	*Tax 50%*	*EAT*	*Ki%(Ki/2)*	*Ke*	*B*	*S = EAT/Ke*	*V = S + B*	*Ko%*
4,00,000	10,000	3,90,000	1,95,000	1,95,000	5.0	0.125	1,00,000	15,47,617	16,47,619	12.13
4,00,000	20,800	3,79,200	1,89,600	1,89,600	5.2	0.13	2,00,000	14,58,461	16,58,461	12.06
4,00,000	33,000	3,67,000	1,83,500	1,83,500	5.5	0.14	3,00,000	13,10,614	16,10,614	12.41
4,00,000	48,000	3,52,000	1,76,000	1,76,000	6.0	0.15	4,00,000	11,73,333	15,73,333	12.71
4,00,000	65,000	3,35,000	1,67,500	1,67,500	6.5	0.17	5,00,000	9,85,294	14,85,294	13.41

$$Ko = \left[Ki \times \frac{B}{V}\right] + \left[Ke \times \frac{S}{V}\right]$$

$$= \left[5 \times \frac{1,00,000}{16,47,619}\right] + \left[12.6 \times \frac{15,47,619}{16,47,619}\right]$$

$= 0.30 + 11.83 = 12.13$ % and so on.

Particulars	*Firm L (Levered)*	*Firm U (Un levered)*
EBIT (20,00,000 × 30%)	6,00,000	6,00,000
Less : Interest(15,00,000 × 12%)	1,80,000	-
EBT	4,20,000	6,00,000
Less : Tax 50%	2,10,000	3,00,000
EAT	2,10,000	3,00,000
Equity Capitalisation Rate (Ke)	0.20	0.20
Market Value of Equity (S = EAT/0.20)	10,50,000	15,00,000
Market value of Debt (B)	15,00,000	-
Total Market value (V = S + B)	25,50,000	15,00,000
Overall capitalisation rate Ko = EBIT/V × 100	23.53	40%

2. Net Operating Income Approach

   a. Value of Unlevered firm (VU):

$$VU = \frac{EBIT(1-T)}{Ke} = \frac{6,00,000(1-0.50)}{0.20}$$

$$= \frac{3,00,000}{0.20} = \text{Rs. } 15,00,000$$

   b. Value of Levered Firm (V1):

$$V1 = VU + Bt = 15,00,000 + 15,00,000\ (0.50)$$

$$= 15,00,000 + 7,50,000 = \text{Rs. } 22,50,000$$

Ko of un levered firm (VU) = 12% (Ke = Ko)

18. Company's U and L are identical in every respect except that the former does not use debt in its capital structure while the latter employees Rs.6,00,000, 10% debt. Assuming that,

    a. All the MM assumption are met,
    b. The corporate tax is 50%.
    c. The EBIT is Rs. 1,20,000 and
    d. The Equity capitalisation of the unlevered company is 12%.

    What will be the value of the firms U and L? Also determine the weighted cost of capital for both the firms.

Solution :

Value of unlevered firm VU:

$$VU = \frac{EBIT(1-T)}{Ke} = \frac{1,20,000(1-0.50)}{0.12}$$

$$= \frac{60,000}{0.12} = \text{Rs. } 5,00,000$$

Value of levered firm (V1):

$$V1 = VU + Bt = 5,00,000 + (6,00,000 \times 0.50)$$

$$= 5,00,000 + 3,00,000 = \text{Rs.}8,00,000$$

Ko of unlevered firm (VU) = 12%, (Ke = Ko)

Ko of levered firm (V1)

EBIT	1,20,000
Less : Interest (6,00,000 × 10%)	60,000
EBT	60,000
Less: Tax 50%	30,000
EAT	30,000
Total market value (v)	8,00,000
Market value of debt (B)	6,00,000
Market value of equity (S) (V – B = S)	2,00,000

$$Ke = \frac{EAT}{S} \times 100 = \frac{30,000}{2,00,000} \times 100 = 15\%$$

$$Ko = \left[Ki \times \frac{B}{V}\right] + \left[Ke \times \frac{S}{V}\right]$$

$$= \left[5 \times \frac{6,00,000}{8,00,000}\right] + \left[15 \times \frac{2,00,000}{8,00,000}\right]$$

$$= 3.75 + 3.75 = 7.50\%$$

19. From the following selected data determine the value of the firms P and Q belonging to the homogeneous risk class under.

a. The Net Income (NI) Approach
b. The Net Operating Income (NOI) Approach

	Levered Firm	*Unlevered Firm*
EBIT	Rs. 2,00,000	Rs, 2,00,000
Interest at 10%	50,000	-
Equity capitalisation rate	15%	
Corporate Tax Rate	50%	

Which of the two firms has an optimal capital structure under the

1. NI Approach
2. NOI Approach

Solution :

1. Valuation of the firm (Net Income Approach)

Particulars	*Firm P (Levered)*	*Firm Q (Unlevered)*
EBIT	2,00,000	2,00,000
Less : Interest	50,000	-
EBT	1,50,000	2,00,000
Less : Tax 50%	75,000	1,00,000
EAT	75,000	1,00,000
Equity Capitalisation rate (Ke)	0.15	0.15
Market value of Equity (S = EAT/Ke)	5,00,000	6,66,667
Market value of Debt (B) (50,000/0.10)	5,00,000	-
Total market value (V = S + B)	10,00,000	6,66,667

Overall cost of capital

$$\text{Firm P (Ko)} = \left[\text{Ki} \times \frac{\text{B}}{\text{V}}\right] + \left[\text{Ke} \times \frac{\text{S}}{\text{V}}\right]$$

$$= \left[5 \times \frac{5,00,000}{10,00,000}\right] + \left[15 \times \frac{50,00,000}{10,00,000}\right]$$

$$= 2.50 + 7.50 = 10\%$$

$$\text{Firm Q (Ko)} = 15\% = \text{Ke}$$

2. Valuation of the firm (Net operating income approach)

$$V_Q = \frac{EBIT(1-T)}{Ke} = \frac{2,00,000(1-0.50)}{0.15} = 6,66,667$$

$$VP = V_Q + B_t = 6,66,667 + (5,00,000 \times 0.50)$$

$$B_p = 6,66,667 + 2,50,000 = 9,16,667$$

$$S_p = V_p - B_p = 9,16,667 - 5,00,000 = Rs.4,16,667$$

$$Ke = \frac{50,000}{4,16,667} = 12\%$$

Firm P

$$Ko = \left[Ki \times \frac{B}{V}\right] + \left[Ke \times \frac{S}{V}\right]$$

$$= \left[5 \times \frac{5,00,000}{9,16,667}\right] + \left[12 \times \frac{6,66,667}{9,16,667}\right]$$

$$= 2.72 + 8.73 = 11.45\%$$

Firm Q (Ko) = 15% = Ke

Firm P has optimal capital structure, both under the NI and NOI Approaches.

20. From the following selected data, determine the value of the firms P and Q belonging to the homogeneous risk class

	Levered Firm P	*Unlevered Firm Q*
EBIT	Rs.2,25,000	Rs. 2,25,000
Interest at 15%	75,000	-
Equity Capitalisation Rate (Ke)	20%	
Corporate Tax rate	50%	

under the net income (NI) approache and Net Operating Income (NOI) Approach.

Which of the two firms has an optimal capital structure under the:

1. NI Approach and 2. NOI Approach

Solution :

Particulars	*Firm P (Levered)*	*Firm Q (Unlevered)*
EBIT	2,25,000	2,25,000
Less: Interest	75,000	-
EBT	1,50,000	2,25,000
Less: Tax 50%	75,000	1,12,500
EAT	75,000	1,12,500
Equity Capitalisation Rate (Ke)	0.20	0.20
Market value of Equity (S = EAT/Ke)	3,75,000	5,62,500
Market value of Debt (B = 75,000/0.15)	5,00,000	-
Total Market Value (V = S + B)	8,75,000	5,62,500

1. Valuation of the firm (NI Approach)

$$\text{Firm P (Ko)} = \left[\text{Ki} \times \frac{B}{V}\right] + \left[\text{Ke} \times \frac{S}{V}\right]$$

$$= \left[7.5 \times \frac{5,00,000}{8,75,000}\right] + \left[20 \times \frac{3,75,000}{8,75,000}\right]$$

$$= 4.29 + 8.57 = 12.86\%$$

Firm Q (Ko) = 20% = Ke.

2. Valuation of the Firm (NOI Approach)

$$V_Q = \frac{\text{EBIT}(1-T)}{\text{Ke}} = \frac{2,25,000(1-0.50)}{0.20} = \text{Rs. } 5,62,500$$

$$V_P = V_Q + B_t = 5,62,500 + (5,00,000 \times 0.50)$$

$$= 5,62,500 + 2,50,000 = \text{Rs. } 8,12,500$$

$$S_P = V_P = B_P = 8,12,500 - 5,00,000 = \text{Rs.} 3,12,500$$

$$\text{Ke} = \frac{\text{EAT}}{S_P} \times 100 = \frac{75,000}{3,12,500} \times 100 = 24\%$$

$$\text{Firm P (Ko)} = \left[\text{Ki} \times \frac{B}{V}\right] + \left[\text{Ke} \times \frac{S}{V}\right]$$

$$= \left[7.5 \times \frac{5,00,000}{8,12,500}\right] + \left[20 \times \frac{3,75,000}{8,12,500}\right]$$

$$= 4.62 + 16.6 = 21.23\%$$

Firm Q (Ko) = 20 = Ke

Firm P has optimal capital structure, both under the NI and NOI Approach.

21. Compute the equilibrium values (V) and equity capitalisation rate of the two companies X and Y on the basis of the data given below. Assume that
    1. There is no income tax
    2. The overall rate of captialisation for such companies in the market is 12.5%

Particulars	*X*	*Y*
Expected Net operating Income (EBIT)	1,50,000	1,50,000
Interest (Ki × B)	20,000	-
NI for equity holders, EBIT - (Ki × B)	1,30,000	1,50,000
Equity capitalisation Rate (Ke)	0.13	0.12
Market value of Equity (S)	10,00,000	12,50,000
Market value of debt (B)	4,00,000	-
Total Market value (V = S + B)	14,00,000	12,50,000
Weighted Average cost of capital (Ko)	10.71%	12%

$$V = \frac{\text{EBIT}}{\text{Ko}} = \frac{1,50,000}{0.125} = \text{Rs. } 12,00,000 \text{ (both for X and Y)}$$

Determination of Ke ?

Solution :

Determination of Equity Capitalisation Rate

Particulars	*X*	*Y*
EBIT	1,50,000	1,50,000
Less : Interest	20,000	-
EBT	1,30,000	1,50,000
Overall Capitalisation Rate (Ko)	0.125	0.125
Total Market value (V = S +B) (V = EBIT/Ko)	12,00,000	12,00,000
Market value of Debt (B)	4,00,000	-
Market value of equity (S)	8,00,000	12,00,000
Equity Capitalisation Rate (Ke)Ke = EBT/S × 100)	16.25%	12.5%

22. The following are the equilibrium values of two firms belonging to the homogeneous risk class according to the NOI approach.

Particulars	*X*	*Y*
Expected net operating income (EBIT)	25,000	25,000
Less Cost of debt (I = Ki × B)	5,000	-
Net income for Equity holders (EBIT-I)	20,000	25,000
Equilibrium cost of capital (Ko)	0.125	0.125
Total value of company (V = EBIT/Ko)	2,00,000	2,00,000
Market value of debt (B)	1,00,000	-
Market value of Equity (V-B)	1,00,000	2,00,000
Cost of Equity (Ke)	20.0%	12.5%

Determine the values of the firms X and Y under the traditional approach, assuming the Ke for company Y as 11% and for X and 14%.

Solution :

Valuation of theVa Firm (Traditional Approach)

Particulars	*X*	*Y*
EBIT	25,000	25,000
Less : Interest	5,000	-
EBT	20,000	25,000
Equity Capitalisation Rate (Ke)	0.14	0.11
Market value of Equity (S = EBT/Ke)	1,42,857	2,27,273
Market value of debt (B)	1,00,000	-
Total Market value (V = S + B)	2,42,857	2,27,273

Overall capitalisation rate (or) overall cost of capital

$$(\text{Ko}) = \frac{\text{EBIT}}{\text{V}} \times 100$$

$$= \frac{25,000}{2,24,857} \times 100$$

$$= 10.29\%$$

$$= \frac{25,000}{2,42,273} \times 100$$

$$= 11\%$$

23. Two Firms A and B are identical in all respects except that the firm A has 10% Rs. 50,000 debentures. Both the firm

have the same earnings before interest and tax amounting to Rs. 10,000. The equity capitalisation rate of firm A is 16% while that of firm B is 12.5%.

You are required to calculate the total market value of each of the firms.

Solution :

Determination of Value of the Firms

Particulars	*Firm A*	*Firm B*
EBIT	10,000	10,000
Less : Interest (50,000 × 10%)	5,000	-
Equity capitalisation Rate (Ke)	0.16	0.125
Market value of Equity (S)	31,250	80,000
Market value of debt (B)	50,000	-
Total Market value (V = S + B)	81,250	80,000
Overall cost of capital (Ko = EBIT/V × 100)	12.3%	12.5%

24. Two firms A and B are identical in all respects except the degree of leverage. Firm A has 6% debt of Rs.3,00,000, While firm B has no debt. Both the firm earnings an EBIT of Rs.1,20,000 each. The equity capilitalisation rate is 10% and the corporate tax is 60%.

    Calculate the market value of the two firms.

Solution :

Particulars	*Firm A*	*Firm B*
EBIT	1,20,000	1,20,000
Less : Interest	18,000	-
EBT	1,02,000	1,20,000
Less: Tax at 60%	61,200	72,000
EAT	40,800	48,000

Value of unlevered Firm B

$$V_U = \frac{EBIT(1-T)}{Ke} = \frac{1,20,000(1-0.60)}{0.10} = \text{Rs. } 4,80,000$$

Value of Levered firm A

$$V1 = VU + Bt = 4{,}80{,}000 + (3{,}00{,}000 \times 0.60)$$
$$= 4{,}80{,}000 + 1{,}80{,}000$$
$$= Rs.6{,}60{,}000$$

25. XY Ltd has an EBIT of Rs.1,00,000. Its cost of debt is 10% and the outstanding debts amounts to Rs.4,00,000. The overall capitalsiation rate is 12.5%. The company decide to raise a sum of Rs.1,00,000 through debt at 10% and uses the proceeds to pay off the equity share holders.

    You are required to calculate the total value of the firm and also the equity capitalisation rate.

Solution :

Determination of Equity Capitalisation Rate

Particulars	*Rs.*
EBIT	1,00,000
Less : Interest (4,00,000 + 1,00,000) × 10%	50,000
EBT	50,000
Overall capitalisation rate (Ko)	0.125
Total Market value (V = S + B)(V = EBIT/Ko)	8,00,000
Market value of debt (B)	5,00,000
Market value of equity (S)	3,00,000

Equity capitalisation Rate (Ke)

$$Ke = \frac{EBT}{S} \times 100 = \frac{50{,}000}{3{,}00{,}000} \times 100 = 16.67\%$$

26. Company X and Y are in the same risk class are identical in every fashion except that company X uses debt while Y does not. The levered firm has Rs.9,00,000 debenture carrying 10% rate of interest. Both the firms earn 20% before interest and taxes on their total assets of Rs.15,00,000. Assume perfect capital market, rational investors and so on a tax rate of 50% for an all equity company. The equity capitalisation rate is 15%.

    1. Compute the value of the firm X and Y using NI Approach
    2. Compute the value of each firm using NOI approach

3. Using NOI approach, overall cost of capital (Ko) for firms X and Y.

Solution :

1. Computation of value of the firm using NI approach

Particulars	*Firm X (Levered)*	*Firm Y (Unlevered)*
EBIT (15,00,000 × 20%)	3,00,000	3,00,000
Less : Interest (9,00,000 × 10%)	90,000	-
EBT	2,10,000	3,00,000
Less : Tax 50%	1,05,000	1,50,000
EAT	1,05,000	1,50,000
Equity capitalisation rate (Ke)	0.15	0.15
Market value of Equity (S) = EBT/Ke	7,00,000	10,00,000
Market value of debt (B)	9,00,000	-
Total value of the firm (V = S + B)	16,00,000	10,00,000

2. Value of the firm using NOI Approach

$$\text{VU (Firm Y)} = \frac{\text{EBIT}(1-\text{T})}{\text{Ke}} = \frac{3,00,000(1-0.50)}{0.15}$$

$$= \frac{1,50,000}{0.15} = \text{Rs.}10,00,000$$

$$\text{V1 (Firm X)} = \text{VU} + \text{Bt} = 10,00,000 + 9,00,000\ (0.50)$$

$$= 10,00,000 + 4,50,000 = \text{Rs. } 14,50,000$$

3. Overall cost of capital using NOI Approach

Company X

EBIT	3,00,000
Less : Interest (9,00,000 × 10%)	90,000
EBT	2,10,000
Less : Tax at 50%	1,05,000
EAT	1,05,000
Total Market value of the firm (V)	14,50,000
Market value of debt (B)	9,00,000

Market value of equity (S = V – B) 5,50,000

$$Ke = \frac{EAT}{S} \times 100 = \frac{1,05,000}{5,50,000} \times 100 = 19.1\%$$

Overall cost of capital (Ko)

$$Ko = \left[Ki \times \frac{B}{V}\right] + \left[Ke \times \frac{S}{V}\right]$$

$$= \left[5 \times \frac{9,00,000}{14,50,000}\right] + \left[19.1 \times \frac{5,50,000}{14,50,000}\right]$$

$$= 3.1 + 7.24 = 10.34\%$$

Company Y

$$Ko = 15.0\% = Ke$$

As a matter of fact according to NOI approach where there are no corporate taxes, every capital structure is optimum. However, in those cases where there are corporate taxes, capital structure will be optimum according to NOI approach. Where there is maximum possible debt content in the capital structure. In view of this none of the firms X and Y has optimum capital structure.

27. Company A and company B are in the same risk class and identical except that A uses debt while B uses equity only. The levered firm A has 10% debentures of Rs.9,00,000. Both the firms earn 20% on their total assets of Rs.15,00,000. the corporate tax rate is 40% and equity capitalisation rate is 15% for an all equity company.
    1. Compute the value of companies A and B using Net Income Approach.
    2. Compute the value of companies A and B using Net Operating Income Approach.
    3. Calculate the overall cost of capital (Ko) for companies A and B

Solution :

1. Computation of value of companies

Particulars	*Company A (Levered)*	*Company B (Unlevered)*
EBIT (15,00,000 × 20%)	3,00,000	3,00,000
Less : Interest (9,00,000 × 10%)	90,000	-
EBT	2,10,000	3,00,000
Less : Tax at 40%	84,000	1,20,000
EAT	1,26,000	1,80,000
Equity Capitalisation Rate (Ke)	0.15	0.15
Market value of Equity (S = EAT/Ke)	8,40,000	12,00,000
Market value of Debt (B)	9,00,000	-
Total Market value (V = S + B)	17,40,000	12,00,000

2. Net Operating Income Approach

$$\text{VU (Firm B)} = \frac{\text{EBIT}(1-\text{T})}{\text{Ke}} = \frac{3,00,000(0.50)}{0.15}$$

$$= \frac{1,50,000}{0.15} = \text{Rs. } 10,00,000$$

$$\text{V1 (Firm A)} = \text{VU} + \text{B}_t = 10,00,000 + 9,00,000\ (0.40)$$

$$= 10,00,000 + 3,60,000 = \text{Rs.}13,60,000$$

3. Overall cost of capital using NOI Approach

Company A:

EBIT	3,00,000
Less : Interest (9,00,000 × 10%)	90,000
EBT	2,10,000
Less : Tax at 40%	84,000
EAT	1,26,000
Total Market value (V)	13,60,000
Market value of Debt (B)	9,00,000
Market value of Equity (S = V – B)	4,60,000

$$\text{Ke} = \frac{\text{EAT}}{\text{S}} \times 100 = \frac{1,26,000}{4,60,000} \times 100 = 27\%$$

Overall cost of capital (Ko)

$$\text{Ko} = \left[\text{Ki} \times \frac{\text{B}}{\text{V}}\right] + \left[\text{Ke} \times \frac{\text{S}}{\text{V}}\right]$$

$$= \left[5 \times \frac{9,00,000}{13,60,000}\right] + \left[27 \times \frac{4,60,000}{13,60,000}\right]$$

$$= 3.31 + 33.8 = 37.11\%$$

Company B:

Ko = 15% = Ke

As a matter of fact according to NOI Approach where there are no corporate taxes, every capital structure is optimum. However, in those cases where there are corporate taxes, capital structure will be optimum according to NOI approach. Where there is maximum possible debt content in the capital structure. In view of this none of the firms A and B has optimum capital structure.

28. Peacock Ltd has earnings before interest and taxes (EBIT) of Rs.72,000. It expects a return on investment of 12%. Find out the value of firm according to the modi gliani – Miller (MM) approach.

Solution :

$$\text{Value of the Firm (V)} = \frac{\text{EBIT}}{\text{Ko}} = \frac{27,000}{\text{Ko}} = \text{Rs. } 6,00,000$$

29. Two firms U and L are identical in all respects except the degree of leverage. Firms U does not use any debt in its financing (unlevered). Firm L has 6% debentures of Rs. 5,00,000 (Levered). The firms have earnings before interest and taxes(EBIT) of Rs.1,50,000 and the equity capitalisation rate is 10%.

Assuming the corporation tax at 40%. Calculate the value of the firm using MM Approach.

Solution :

a. Value of unlevered firm

EBIT	1,50,000
Less: Tax (1,50,000 × 40%)	60,000
EAT	90,000

Equity capitalisation Rate (Ke) = 10%

Value of unlevered Firm (VU) $= \frac{EAT}{Ke}$

$$= \frac{90,000}{0.10} = \text{Rs. } 9,00,000$$

b. Value of levered Firm (V1)

V1 = Vu + Bt = 9,00,000 + (5,00,000 × 0.40)

= 9,00,000 + 2,00,000 = Rs.11,00,000

30. Two firms X and Y are identical except in the method of financing, Firm X has while from Y has Rs. 2,00,000 5% debentures in financing. Both the firms have a net operating income (EBIT) of Rs. 50,000 and equity cpaitalisation rate of 12.5%. The corporate tax rate is 50%. Calculate the value of the firm using MM approach.

Solution :

a. Value of unlevered firm (VU)

Firm X

EBIT	50,000
Less: Tax at 50%	25,000
EAT	25,000

Equity cpaitalisation rate (Ke) = 12.5%

$$VU = \frac{EAT}{Ke} = \frac{25,000}{0.125} = \text{Rs. } 2,00,000$$

b. Value of levered firm (V1)

Firm Y

V1 = VU + Bt = 2,00,000 + (2,00,000 × 0.50)

= 2,00,000 + 1,00,000 = Rs. 3,00,000

31. Firm A and B are identical in every respect except that A is unlevered while B is levered company. Company B has Rs.20,00,000 of 9% debentures outstanding. Assume

1. That all the MM assumptions are met
2. That the tax rate is 50%

3. That the EBIT is Rs. 4,00,000 and the equity capitalisation rate for company B is 10%
   a. Find the value of each firm under the MM approach
   b. Suppose the value of firm A (unlevered) is Rs. 15,00,000 and value of Firm B (levered) is Rs. 34,00,000, do they represent equilibrium values according to MM? If not, explain the process by which equilibrium will be reached. No calculations are required.

Solution :

Value of unlevered firm (VU)

Firm A

EBIT	4,00,000
Less: Tax 50%	2,00,000
EAT	2,00,000

$$\text{Value of unlevered firm (VU)} = \frac{\text{EAT}}{\text{Ke}}$$

$$= \frac{2,00,000}{0.10} = \text{Rs. } 20,00,000$$

Value of Levered Firm (V1):

Firm B :

$$\text{V1} = \text{VU} + \text{Bt} = 20,00,000 + (20,00,000 \times 0.50)$$

$$= 20,00,000 + 10,00,000 = \text{Rs. } 30,00,000$$

Chapter 5

CAPITAL BUDGETING

Meaning

The term "Capital budgeting refers to long term planning for proposed capital out lays and there financing capital budgeting is the process of making investment decision in capital expenditure. A capital expenditure may be defined as an expenditure, the benefits of which are expected to be received over a period of time exceeding one year.

Definition

According to Hampton, capital budgeting maybe defined as "The firms formal process for the acquisition and investment of capital".

Need and significance of Capital Budgeting

The need and significance or importance of capital budgeting arrises mainly due to the following reasons.

i. Large investments

ii. Permanent commitment of funds

iii. Irreversible in nature

iv. Long term effect on profitability

v. Difficulties of investment decisions

vi. National importance

Steps Involved in Capital Budgeting

The following steps are involved.

1. Creative search for profitable opportunities
2. Long range capital plans
3. Short range capital budget
4. Measurement of project worth
5. Screening and selection
6. Establishing priorities
7. Final approval
8. Forms and procedures
9. Retirement and disposal
10. Evaluation

Kinds of Capital Investment Projects

1. Profit earning projects
   a. Improving quality of products
   b. Research and development
   c. Improving facilities
   d. Cost reduction and cost improvement
   e. Maintenance of earnings
2. Non – Profit project
3. Projects the profitability of which cannot be measured.

Methods of Capital Budgeting

1. Pay back period method
2. Accounting rate of return method
3. Discounted cash flow method
   a. Net present value method
   b. Excess present value index method
   c. Internal rate of return method

1. *Pay back period method:* Pay back method is popularly known as pay off, pay out method. It is defined as the number of years required to recover initial cash out lay invested in a project.

$$\text{Computation of pay back period} = \frac{\text{Initial investment}}{\text{Annual cash inf lows}}$$

Merits of Pay Back Period Method

i. It is easy to understand
ii. It is simple to operate
iii. It is useful where profitability is not important
iv. It is useful where the business is suffering from shortage of funds as quick recovery is essential for repayment
v. It is useful for industries.

Demerits of Pay Back Period Method

i. This is delicate and rigid
ii. Asset individually in issolation
iii. Wastage
iv. Profitability is completely ignored
v. Ignores time value of money

2. *Accounting rate of return method:* This method is also known as average rate of return method (ARR) or financial statement method or unadjusted rate of return method or book value method.

   It takes into account, the accounting concept its profit (ie profit after depreciation and tax) and not the cash inflows.

   The project which yield the highest rate of return is selected. The rate of return means the average annual return on a project.

$$\text{ARR } \frac{\text{Average Pr ofit}}{\text{Original investment}} \times 100$$

$$\text{or } \frac{\text{Average Pr ofit}}{\text{Average investment}} \times 100$$

Merits of ARR Method

i. It is simple and easy to understand
ii. Entire economic life

iii. Weight to the profitability of the project
iv. Simple rate of return

Demerits of ARR Method

i. Different methods are inconsistent
ii. Very critical in business decisions
iii. Fair rate of return and investment
iv. Simple average technique

3. *Discounted cash flow method:* The discounted cash flow method is an improvement on the pay back method. This method takes into account the profitability and also the time value of money. These methods are also called modern methods of capital budgeting and becoming increasingly popular day by day. Discounted investment proposals are of three types.
    1. Net present value method
    2. Excess present value index
    3. Internal rate of return
    1. *Net present value method (NPV):* Under this method, present value of cash inflows in calculated at the required rate of return and compared with the original investment. If the present value is higher than the original investment, the project can be selected otherwise rejected.
    2. *Excess present value index:* One of the major disadvantages of the present value method is that it is not easy to rank projects on the basis of net present value when the cost of the projects differ. To compare such projects the present value index is prepared. It can be calculated with the help of the following formula.

    Excess Present value index

$$\frac{\text{Total Present value of cash inflows}}{\text{Total Present Value of Cash outflows}}$$

3. *Internal rate of return (IRR):* IRR is the rate of return at which total present value of future cash inflows is equal to initial investment. This method is used when the cost of investment and cash inflows are known but the rate of return is unknown. The rate of return is generally found by trial and error method.

Merits of Discounted Cash flow Method

i. It considers the time value of money.

ii. It considers income over the entire life of the product

iii. It provides comparison between projects

iv. It is the best method where cash inflows are uneven

v. This approach recognizes time factor.

Demerits of Discounted Cash flow Method

i. Some argue that this method is too difficult to use.

ii. The selection of an appropriate rate of interest is also difficult.

iii. It does not correspond to accounting concepts for regarding revenues.

iv. It is very difficult to forecast the economic life of any investment exactly.

Practical Problems

Pay Back Period Method

1. A protect costs Rs.1,00,000 and yields an annual cash inflow of Rs.20,000 for 7 years. Calculate the pay back period.

Solution :

$$\text{Pay back period} = \frac{\text{Initial Investment}}{\text{annual Cash Inflow}} = \frac{1,00,000}{20,000}$$

$$= 5 \text{ yeary}$$

2. Calculate pay back period for a project which requires a cash out lay of Rs. 10,000 and generates cash out lay of

Rs. 2,000, Rs. 4,000, Rs. 3,000 and Rs. 2,000 in the first, second, third and fourth year respectively.

Solution :

Year	*Cash inflows Rs.*	*Cumulative cashinflows Rs.*
1	2,000	2,000
2	4,000	6,000
3	3,000	9,000
4	2,000	11,000

Pay back period = 3 years and 6 months

Workings:

$$10{,}000 - 9{,}000 = 1{,}000$$

$$11{,}000 - 9{,}000 = 2{,}000$$

$$\frac{1{,}000}{2{,}000} \times 12 \text{ months} = 6 \text{ months.}$$

3. A project cost Rs.5,00,000 and yields annually a profit of Rs.80,000 after depreciation at 12% P.a. but before tax of 50%. Calculate the pay back period.

Solution :

$$\text{Pay back period} = \frac{\text{Initial Investment}}{\text{Annual cash inflow}}$$

Initial Investment – Rs.5,00,000

Annual cash inflow = profit after tax + Depreciation

Profit before tax	= 80,000
Less: Tax (80,000x50%)	= 40,000
Profit after tax	= 40,000
Add: Depreciation (5,00,000x12%)	= 60,000
Annual cash inflow	= 1,00,000

Pay back period $= \frac{5{,}00{,}000}{1{,}00{,}000} = 5$ years.

4. There are two projects A and B. The cost of the project is Rs.30,000 in each case. The cash inflows are as under.

Year	*Cash inflows Rs.*	
	Project A	*Project B*
1	10,000	2,000
2	10,000	4,000
3	10,000	24,000

Solution :

Calculate Pay Back Period

Year	*Project A*		*Project B*	
	Cash inflows Rs.	*Cumulative cash inflows Rs.*	*Cash inflowsRs.*	*Cumulative cashinflows Rs.*
1	10,000	10,000	2,000	2,000
2	10,000	20,000	4,000	6,000
3	10,000	30,000	24,000	30,000

The pay back period is 3 years in both the cases. However, project A is better compared to project B because cash inflows are greater in the initial years.

5. Siva Ltd., is considering two projects X and Y each costing Rs.20,000. The net cash flows from the projects are as follows.

Year	*1*	*2*	*3*	*4*	*5*	*6*
X (Rs)	10,000	8,000	6,000	2,000	-	-
Y (Rs.)	2,000	4,000	6,000	8,000	8,000	9,000

The company has fixed three years as the cut off period. State which project should be accepted ?

Solution :

Year	*Project X*		*Project Y*	
	Cash inflows Rs.	*Cumulative cash inflows Rs.*	*Cash inflowsRs.*	*Cumulative cashinflows Rs.*
1	10,000	10,000	2,000	2,000
2	8,000	18,000	4,000	6,000
3	6,000	24,000	6,000	12,000
4	2,000	26,000	8,000	20,000
5	-	26,000	8,000	28,000
6	-	26,000	9,000	37,000

Pay Back Period

Project X = 2 years and 4 month

20,000 – 18,000 = 2,000

24,000 –1800 = 6,000 × 12 months = 4 months

Project Y = 4 years

Project X is preferable as it has a shorter pay back period.

6. An organization has a cut off pay back period of 3 years and 6 months. Advise the company with regard to the following exclusive investments.

Project	*Total investment Rs.*	*Annual cash inflow Rs.*	*Period of inflow*
A	50000	15000	4 years
B	80000	24000	5 years
C	80000	20000	6 years
D	40000	12000	5 years
E	10000	1800	7 years

Solution :

$$\text{Pay back period} = \frac{\text{Inital Investment}}{\text{Annual cash inf low}}$$

A = 50,000 ÷ 15,000 = 3 years and 4 months

B = 80,000 ÷ 24,000 = 3 years and 4 months

C = 80,000 ÷ 20,000 = 4 months

D = 40,000 ÷ 12,000 = 3 years and 4 months

E = 10,000 ÷ 18,000 = 5 years and 7 months

The cut off pay back period is 3 years and 4 months. Project A, B and D may be considered as they have a pay back period of 3 years and 4 months. Of these D and B are better as post pay back cash inflow is available for 1 year and 8 months (5 years - 3 years and 4 months). In the case of A, post pay back cash inflow is available only for 8 months (4 years - 3 years and 4 months).

7. A company proposing to expand its production can go in either for an automatic machine costing Rs. 2,24,000 with

an estimated life of 5½ years or an ordinary machine costing Rs. 60,000 having an estimated life of 8 years. The annual sales and costs are estimated as follows.

	Automatic Machine Rs.	*Ordinary Machine Rs.*
Sale	1,50,000	1,50,000
Costs		
Material	50,000	50,000
Labour	12,000	60,000
Variable overheads	24,000	20,000

Compute the comparative profitability of the proposals under the pay back method. Ignore income tax.

Solution :

Profitability Statement

Particulars	*Automatic Machine Rs.*	*Ordinary Machine Rs.*
Cost of the Machine	2,24,000	60,000
Sales	1,50,000	1,50,000
Less : Cost (Material + labour + overhead)	86,000	1,30,000
Annual cash inflow	64,000	20,000

$$\text{Pay back period} = \frac{2,24,000}{64,000} \qquad = \frac{60,000}{20,000}$$

$$= 3\tfrac{1}{2}\text{ years} \qquad = 3\text{ years}$$

Profitability Beyond Pay Back

= 64,000 × 2 (5½ years – 3½ years) = Rs.1,28,000

= 20,000 × 5 (8 years – 3 years) = Rs. 1,00,000

From the view point of pay back period alone, ordinary machine having a shorter pay back period should be recommended. But if we consider the full serviceable life of asset, automatic machine is preferable because it gives a surplus of Rs. 1,28,000 in 5½ years while the ordinary machine gives a surplus of only Rs. 1,00,000 in 8 years.

8. A company has to choose one of the following two mutually exclusive projects. Investment required for each project is Rs.15,000. Both the projects have to be depreciated on straight line basis. The tax rate is 50%.

Calculate Pay Back Period

Year	*Profit before depreciation*	
	Project A	*Project B*
1	4,200	4,200
2	4,800	4,500
3	7,000	4,000
4	7,000	5,000
5	2,000	10,000

Solution :

$$\text{Depreciation} = \frac{15,000}{5\,\text{years}} = 3,000 \text{ for A and B}$$

Project A

Years	*Profit*	*Less: Deprn*	*Profit After*	*Tax 50%*	*Profit After*	*Add: Deprn*	*Cash inflow*	*Cumulative cash inflow*
1	4200	3000	1200	600	600	3000	3600	3600
2	4800	3000	1800	900	900	3000	3900	7500
3	7000	3000	4000	2000	2000	3000	5000	12500
4	7000	3000	4000	2000	2000	3000	5000	17500
5	2000	3000	-1000	-	-1000	3000	2000	19500

Pay back period = 3 years and 6 months

15,000 – 12,500 = 2,500

$$17,500 - 12,500 = 5,000 \quad \frac{2,500}{5,000} \times 12 \text{ months} = 6 \text{ months}$$

Project B

Years	*Profit*	*Less: Deprn*	*Profit After*	*Tax 50%*	*Profit After*	*Add: Deprn*	*Cash inflow*	*Cumulative cash inflow*
1	4200	3000	1200	600	600	3000	3600	3600
2	4500	3000	1500	750	750	3000	3750	7350

Contd...

Years	*Profit*	*Less: Deprn*	*Profit After*	*Tax 50%*	*Profit After*	*Add: Deprn*	*Cash inflow*	*Cumulative cash inflow*
3	4000	3000	1000	500	500	3000	3500	10850
4	5000	3000	2000	1000	1000	3000	4000	14850
5	10000	3000	7000	3500	3500	3000	6500	21350

Pay back period = 4 years and 8 days

15,000 - 14,850 = 150

21,350 - 14,850 = 6,500

$$\frac{150}{6,500} \times 365 \text{ days} = 8 \text{ days}$$

Project A is a preferable as it has a shorter pay back period.

Note : Below 1000 (Top Amount) is 365 days.
Above 1000 (Top amount) is 12 months.

9. A Ltd., is producing articles mostly by manual labour and is considering to replace it by a new machine. There are two alternative models X and Y of the new machine. Prepare a statement of profitability showing the pay back period from the following information. Ignore taxation.

	Machine X	*Machine Y*
Estimated life of machine	4 years	5 years
Cost of machine	Rs. 9,000	18,000
Estimated savings in Scrap	Rs.500	800
Estimated saving in direct wages	Rs.6,000	8,000
Additional cost of maintenance	Rs,800	1,000
Additional cost of supervision	Rs.1,200	1,800

Solution :

Particulars	*Machine X Rs.*	*Machine Y Rs.*
Estimated saving in scrap	500	800
Estimated saving in Direct wages	6,000	8,000
Total saving (A)	6,500	8,800
Additional Cost of Maintenance	800	1000
Additional cost of supervision	1200	1800
Total Additional cost (B)	2000	2800
Net cash inflow (A-B)	4500	6000

$$\text{Pay back period} = \frac{\text{Original Investment}}{\text{annual Cash inflow}}$$

$$= \frac{9,000}{4,500} = 2 \text{ years} \quad \frac{18,000}{6,000} = 3 \text{ years}$$

Machine X should be preferred because it has a shorter pay back period.

10. Rex Ltd., is considering the purchase of a new machine which will carryout the operations performed by labour. Damsel and Shylock are alternative model. From the following information, you are required to prepare a profitability statement and workout the pay back period in respect of each machine.

	Machine Damsel Rs.	*Machine Shylock Rs.*
Estimated life of machine (years)	10	12
Cost of machine	3,00,000	5,00,000
Cost of indirect material p.a	12,000	16,000
Estimated saving in scrap p.a	20,000	30,000
Additional cost of maintenance p.a.	14,000	22,000
Additional cost of supervision p.a.	24,000	32,000
Estimated savings in direct wages:-		
Employees not required (number)	150	200
Wages per employees p.a.	1200	1200

Taxation is to be regarded as 50% of profit (ignore depreciation for calculation of tax). Which model would you recommended.

Solution :

Profitability Statement

	Machine Damsel Rs.		*Machine Shylock Rs.*	
	Rs.	*Rs.*	*Rs.*	*Rs.*
Estimated Savings in scrap p.a	20,000		30,000	
Estimated savings in direct wages (1200 × 150, 1200 × 200)	1,80,000		2,40,000	

Contd...

	Machine Damsel Rs.		*Machine Shylock Rs.*	
	Rs.	*Rs.*	*Rs.*	*Rs.*
Total Savings		2,00,000		2,70,000
Less : Additional Cost p.a :-				
Indirect Material	12,000		16,000	
Supervision	24,000		32,000	
Maintenance	14,000		22,000	
Total Additional Cost		50,000		70,000
Savings before depreciation		1,50,000		2,00,000
Less : Tax at 50%		75,000		1,00,000
Annual cash inflow		75,000		1,00,000

$$\text{Pay back period} = \frac{\text{Initial Investment}}{\text{annual Cash inf low}}$$

$$= \frac{3,00,000}{75,000} = 4 \text{ years}, \frac{5,00,000}{1,00,000} = 5 \text{ years}$$

Machine Damsel is preferable because it has a shorter pay back period.

11. For each of the following projects calculate a. pay back period, b. Post pay back profitability and c. Post pay back profitability index.

I.	Initial outlay	Rs. 1,00,000
	Annual Cash inflow	Rs. 20,000
II.	Initial outlay	Rs. 60,000
	Annual Cash inflows for first 3 years	Rs. 15,000
	Annual Cash inflows for next 5 years	Rs. 5,000
	Estimated life 8 years	
	Salvage value	Rs. 8,000

Solution :

I. a. $\text{Pay back period} = \frac{\text{Initial Investment}}{\text{Annual Cash inf low}}$

$$= \frac{1,00,000}{5,00,000} = 5 \text{ years}$$

b. Post pay back profitability

= Annual Cash inflows × (Estimated life-pay back period)

= 20,000 (8 - 5) = 20,000 × 3 = Rs.60,000

c. Post pay back profitability index

$$= \frac{\text{Post pay back profit}}{\text{Initial investment}} \times 100$$

$$= \frac{60,000}{1,00,000} \times 100 = 60\%$$

II. a. Pay back period

Year	*Annual cash. inflows Rs*	*Cumulative Cash inflows Rs.*
1	15,000	15,000
2	15,000	30,000
3	15,000	45,000
4	5,000	50,000
5	5,000	55,000
6	5,000	60,000
7	5,000	65,000
8	5,000	70,000

Pay back period = 6 years

b. Post pay back profitability = 5,000 × (8 -6)

= Rs. 5000 × 2 = Rs. 10,000

c. Post pay back profitability index $= \frac{10,000}{60,000} \times 100 = 16.67\%$

12. Calculate discounted pay back period from the following information.

Cost of the project = Rs. 3,00,000

Life of the project = 5 years

Annual Cash inflow = Rs. 1,00,000

Year	*1*	*2*	*3*	*4*	*5*
P.V. Factor @10%	0.909	0.826	0.751	0.683	0.621

Solution :

Statement Showing Present Value of Cash Inflows

Year	Cash inflows	P.V. factor @10%	Present value of cash inflows	Cumulative cash inflows
1	1,00,000	0.909	90,900	90,900
2	1,00,000	0.826	82,600	1,73,500
3	1,00,000	0.751	75,100	2,48,600
4	1,00,000	0.683	68,300	3,16,900
5	1,00,000	0.621	62,100	3,79,000

Discounted pay back period

= 3 years and 9 months

= 3,00,000 – 2,48,600 = 51,400

= 3,16,900 – 2,48,000 = 68,300

$$= \frac{51,400}{68,300} \times 12 \text{ months} = 9 \text{ months}$$

13. Calculate the pay back periods of the following projects each requiring a cash outlay of Rs. 1,00,000. Suggest which projects are acceptable, if the standard pay back period is 5 years.

Year	Cash inflows		
	Project A	*Project B*	*Project C*
1	30,000	30,000	10,000
2	30,000	40,000	20,000
3	30,000	20,000	30,000
4	30,000	10,000	40,000
5	30,000	5,000	-

Solution :

Computation of Pay Back Period

Year	Project A		Project B		Project C	
	Cash	Cumulative	Cash	Cumulative	Cash	Cumulative
1	30,000	30,000	30,000	30,000	10,000	10,000
2	30,000	60,000	40,000	70,000	20,000	30,000
3	30,000	90,000	20,000	90,000	30,000	60,000
4	30,000	1,20,000	10,000	1,00,000	40,000	1,00,000
5	30,000	1,50,000	5,000	1,05,000	-	1,00,000

Pay back period

Project A = 3 years and 4 months

Project B = 4 years

Project C = 4 years

Workings :

1,00,000 – 90,000 = 10,000

1,20,000 – 90,000 = 30,000

$$\frac{10,000}{30,000} \times 12 \text{ months} = 4 \text{ months}$$

Project A is preferable as it has a shorter pay back period.

NET PRESENT VALUE METHOD OR DISCOUNTED CASH FLOW METHOD

14. Project X initially costs Rs.25,000. It generates the following cash inflows.

Year	*Cash inflows Rs.*	*Present Value of Re.1 at 10%*
1	9,000	0.909
2	8,000	0.826
3	7,000	0.751
4	6,000	0.683
5	5,000	0.621

Taking the cut off rate as 10%, suggest whether the project should be accepted or not.

Solution :

Year	*Cash inflows Rs.*	*Present value factor at 10%*	*Present value of cash inflows Rs.*
1	9,000	0.909	8,181
2	8,000	0.826	6,608
3	7,000	0.751	5,257
4	6,000	0.683	4,098
5	5,000	0.621	3,105
Total Present value of cash inflows			27,249
Less: Total Present Value of cash outflows			25,000
Net present Value (NPV)			2,249

As net present value is positive, the project is recommended.

15. Calculate the net present value at 10%
    Estimated life of the machine – 3 years
    Capital cost – Rs. 10,000
    Net earnings after tax

Year	Rs.	P.V. Factor at 10%
1	8000	0.909
2	6000	0.826
3	4000	0.751

Solution :

Computation of Net Present Value

Year	Cash inflows Rs.	Present value factor at 10%	Present value of cash inflows Rs.
1	8000	0.909	7272
2	6000	0.826	4956
3	4000	0.751	3004
Total present value of cash inflows			15232
Less : Total present value of cash outflows			10,000
Net Present value (NPV)			5,232

Net present value is positive. Therefore, the machine is recommended.

16. The initial cash out lay of a project is Rs. 50,000. Estimates cash inflows.

Compute Profitability Index

Year	Rs.	P.V. Factor at 10%
1	20000	0.909
2	15000	0.826
3	25000	0.751
4	10000	0.683

As net present value is positive, the project is recommended.

Solution :

Year	*Cash inflows Rs.*	*Present value factor at 10%*	*Present value of cash inflows Rs.*
1	20,000	0.909	18,180
2	15,000	0.826	12,390
3	25,000	0.751	18,775
4	10,000	0.683	6,830
Total Present value of cash inflows			56,175
Less : Total Present value of cash outflows			50,000
Net Present value (NPV)			6,175

17. The financial manager of a company has to advice the board of directors on choosing between two compelling project proposals which require on equal investment of Rs. 1,00,000 and are expected to generate cash flows as under.

	Project I Rs.	*Project II*
End of I year	48,000	20,000
End of II year	32,000	24,000
End of III year	20,000	36,000
End of IV year	Nil	48,000
End of V year	24,000	16,000
End of VI year	12,000	8,000

Which project proposals should be recommended and why? Assume the cost of capital to be 10% p.a. The following are the present value factors at 10% p.a.

Year	*1*	*2*	*3*	*4*	*5*	*6*
Factor	0.909	0.826	0.751	0.683	0.621	0.564

Solution :

Computation of Net Present Value

Year	*P.V. Factorat 10%*	*Project I Cashin inflows*	*Project I Total P.V. of cash inflows*	*Project II Cash inflows*	*Project II Total P.V. of Cash inflows*
1	0.909	48,000	43,632	20,000	18,180
2	0.826	32,000	26,432	24,000	19,824
3	0.751	20,000	15,020	36,000	27,036
4	0.683	-	-	48,000	32,784

Contd...

Year	P.V. Factorat 10%	Project I Cashin inflows	Project I Total P.V. of cash inflows	Project II Cash inflows	Project II Total P.V. of Cash inflows
5	0.621	24,000	14,904	16,000	9,936
6	0.564	12,000	6,768	8,000	4,512
Total present value of cash inflows			106756		1,12,272
Less : Total Present value of cash outflows			1,00,000	1,00,000	
Net present value (NPV)			6,756		12,272

Project II is preferable because it has a higher net present value.

18. The Directors of A Ltd., Consider a proposal to invest a sum of Rs. 1,00,000 on plant that has an expected life of 5 years which at the end has no residual value.

The expected annual income during the life of the plant are:

	Rs.
I year	30,000
II year	40,000
III year	40,000
IV year	30,000
V year	20,000
	1,60,000

Money is available at an interest of 10% p.a. calculate the net present value.

Solution :

Computation of Net Present Value

Year	Present value factor at 10%	Present value of cash inflows	Total present value of cash inflows
I	0.909	30,000	27,270
II	0.826	40,000	33,040
III	0.751	40,000	30,040
IV	0.683	30,000	20,490
V	0.621	20,000	12,420
Total present value of cash inflows			1,23,260
Less: Total present value of cash outflows			1,00,000
Net Present value (NPV)			23,260

As the net present value is positive. Therefore, the proposal is recommended.

19. The Alpha Co. Ltd., is considering the purchase of a new machine. Two alternative machine (A and B) have been suggested, each having an initial cost of Rs. 4,00,000 and requiring Rs. 20,000 as additional working capital at the end of first year. Earnings after taxation are expected to be as follows.

Year	*Cash inflows*	
	Machine A	*Machine B*
1	40,000	1,20,000
2	1,20,000	1,60,000
3	1,60,000	2,00,000
4	2,40,000	1,20,000
5	1,60,000	80,000

The company has a target of return on capital of 10% and on this basis, you are required to compare the profitability of the machines and state which alternative you consider financially preferable ?

Note : The following table gives the present value of Re.1 due in "n" number of years.

Year	*1*	*2*	*3*	*4*	*5*
P.V. Factor at 10%	0.91	0.83	0.75	0.68	0.62

Solution :

Statement Showing Net Present Values

Year	*Present value factor at 10%*	*Machine A*		*Machine B*	
		Cash inflows	*Total present value cahs inflows*	*Cash inflows Rs.*	*Total Present value cash inflows Rs*
1	0.91	40,000	36,400	1,20,000	1,09,200
2	0.83	1,20,000	99,600	1,60,000	1,32,800
3	0.75	1,60,000	1,20,000	2,00,000	1,50,000
4	0.68	2,40,000	1,63,200	1,20,000	81,600
5	0.62	1,60,000	99,200	80,000	49,600
Total PV of cash inflows		5,18,400		5,23,200	

Contd...

20TH SUM ANSWER

Year	P.V. Factor at 10%	Project A		Project B		Project C		Project D		Project E		Project F	
		Cash Inflows	T.P Value Cash Inflows	Cash Inflows	T.P Value Cash Inflows	Cash Inflows	T.P Value Cash Inflows	Cash Inflows	T.P Value Cash Inflows	Cash Inflows	T.P Value Cash Inflows	Cash Inflows	T.P Value Cash Inflows
1	0.909	2,00,000	1,81,800	1,00,000	90,000	20,000	18,180	2,00,000	1,81,800	1,40,000	1,27,260,	1,60,000	1,45,440
2.	0.825	-	-	1,00,000	82,600	1,00,000	82,600	2,00,00	16,520	60,000	49,560	46,560	1,32,160
3.	0.751	-	-	1,00,000	75,100	3,00,000	2,25,300	20,000	15,020	1,00,000	75,100	75,100	60,080
Total P.V. of Cash outflows			1,81,800		2,48,600		3,26,080		2,13,340		2,51,920		3,37680
Less: Total PV of Cash outflow			2,00,000		2,00,000		2,00,000		2,00,000		2,00,000		2,00,000
Net Present Value (NPV)			-18,200		48,600		1,26800		13,340		15,920		1,37,680

Project f is recommended Because it has greater net present value.

Year	*Present value factor at 10%*	*Machine A*		*Machine B*	
		Cash inflows	*Total present value cahs inflows*	*Cash inflows Rs.*	*Total Present value cash inflows Rs.*
Less: Total P.V. of cash outflows (4,00,000 + 20000 × 0.91)		4,18,200			4,18,200
Net Present Value		1,00,200			1,05,000

Machine B is preferable as it has a higher net present value.

20. Consider the following proposed investments with the indicated cash inflows.

	Investment	*Initial outlay Year 1 (Rs. 000) (Rs. 000)*	*Year – end Cash inflows* Year 2 (Rs. 000)	Year 3 (Rs. 000)
A	200	200	Nil	Nil
B	200	100	100	100
C	200	20	100	300
D	200	200	20	20
E	200	140	60	100
F	200	160	160	80

Rank the investments deriving the net present value (NPV) using a discount rate of 10% and state your views.

Year	*1*	*2*	*3*
P.V. Factor at 10%	0.909	0.826	0.751

21. A choice is to be made between two competing proposals which require an capital investment of Rs.50,000 and are expected to generate net cash flows as under:

	Project I	*Project II*
End of the year 1	Rs. 25,000	Rs. 10,000
End of the year 2	15,000	12,000
End of the year 3	10,000	18,000
End of the year 4	Nil	25,000
End of the year 5	12,000	8,000
End of the year 6	6,000	4,000

The cost of capital of the company is 10%. The following are the presented value factors at 10% p.a.

Year	*1*	*2*	*3*	*4*	*5*	*6*
PV factor at 10%	0.909	0.826	0.751	0.683	0.621	0.564

Which project proposal should be chosen and why?

Evaluate the project proposal under:

a. Pay back period

b. Discounted cash flow method

c. Excess present value index

Solution :

a. Pay back period method

Year	*Project I*		*Project II*	
	Cash inflows	*Cumulative cash inflows*	*Cash inflows*	*Cumulative cash inflows*
1	25,000	25,000	10,000	10,000
2	15,000	40,000	12,000	22,000
3	10,000	50,000	18,000	40,000
4	-	50,000	25,000	65,000
5	12,000	62,000	8,000	73,000
6	6,000	68,000	4,000	77,000

Pay back period

Project I = 3 years

Project II = 3 years and 5 months

50,000 – 40,000 = 10,000

65,000 – 40,000 = 25,000

$$\frac{10,000}{25,000} \times 12 \text{ months} = 5 \text{ months}$$

Project I is preferable because it has shorter pay back period.

b. Discount cash flow method

Year	*P.V. Factor at 10%*	*Project I*		*Project II*	
		Cash inflows	*Cumulative cash inflows*	*Cash inflows*	*Cumulative cash inflows*
1	0.909	25,000	22,725	10,000	9,090
2	0.826	15,000	12,390	12,000	9,912
3	0.751	10,000	7,510	18,000	13,518
4	0.683	-	-	25,000	17,075
5	0.621	12,000	7,452	8,000	4,968
6	0.564	6,000	3,384	4,000	2,256
T.P. Value of cash inflows			53,461		56,819
Less: TP Value of cash outflows			50,000		50,000
Net Present value (NPV)			3,461		6,819

As net present value is greater in project II, it is preferable.

c. Excess present value index

$$\frac{\text{Total Present value of Cash inflows}}{\text{Total present Value of cash outflows}} = \times 100$$

$$\text{Project I} = \frac{53,461}{50,000} \times 100 = 107\ \%$$

$$\text{Project II} = \frac{56,819}{50,000} \times 100 = 114\ \%$$

22. The following are the cash inflows and outflows of a certain project.

Year	*Outflows*	*Inflow*
0	1,50,000	-
1	30,000	30,000
2	-	30,000
3	-	50,000
4	-	60,000
5	-	40,000

The salvage value at the end of 5 years is Rs.40,000. Taking the cut off rate as 10% calculate net present value.

Year	1	2	3	4	5
PV Factor at 10%	0.909	0.826	0.751	0.683	0.621

Solution :

Computation of Net Present Value

Year	*Present value factor at 10%*	*Present value cash inflows* (Rs.)	*Total Present value of cash inflows (Rs.)*
1	0.909	30,000	27,270
2	0.826	30,000	24,780
3	0.751	50,000	37,750
4	0.683	60,000	40,980
5	0.621	40,000	24,840
6	0.621	40,000 [salvage]	24,840
Total Present Value of Cash inflows			1,80,260
Less: Total present Value of cash outflows			1,77,270
Net Present Value (NPV)			2,990

Net present value is positive, therefore, the project is recommended.

23. The financial manager of a company has to advise the board of directors on choosing between two compelling project proposals which require on equal investment of Rs.1,00,000 and are expected to generate cash flows as under:

	Project I	*Project II*
End of year 1	48,000	20,000
End of year 2	32,000	24,000
End of year 3	20,000	36,000
End of year 4	Nil	48,000
End of year 5	24,000	16,000
End of year 6	12,000	8,000

Which project proposal should be recommended and why? Assume the cost of capital to be 10% p. a. The following are the present value factors at 10% p. a.

Year	1	2	3	4	5	6
Factor	0.909	0.826	0.751	0.683	0.621	0.564

Evaluate the project proposals under

a. Pay back period
b. Discount cash flow method
c. Excess present value index

Solution :

a. Pay back period method

Year	Project I		Project II	
	Cash inflows Rs.	Cumulative cash inflows Rs.	Cash inflows Rs.	Cumulative cash inflows Rs.
1	48,000	48,000	20,000	20,000
2	32,000	80,000	24,000	44,000
3	20,000	1,00,000	36,000	80,000
4	-	1,00,000	48,000	1,28,000
5	24,000	1,24,000	16,000	1,44,000
6	12,000	1,36,000	8,000	1,52,000

Pay back period

Project I = 3 years

Project II = 3 years and 5 months

1,00,000 – 80,000 = 20,000

1,28,000 – 80,000 = 48,000

$$\frac{20,000}{48,000} \times 12 \text{ month} = 5 \text{ months}$$

Project I is preferable because it has a shorter pay back period.

b. Discounted cash flow method

Year	P.V. Factor at 10%	Project I		Project II	
		Cash inflows	T.P. value of cash inflows	Cash inflows	T.P. value of cash inflows
1	0.909	48,000	43,632	20,000	18,180
2	0.826	32,000	26,432	24,000	19,824

Contd...

Year	*P.V. Factor at 10%*	*Project I*		*Project II*	
		Cash inflows	*T.P.value of cash inflows*	*Cash inflows*	*T.P.value of cash inflows*
3	0.751	20,000	15,020	36,000	27,036
4	0.683	-	-	48,000	32,784
5	0.621	24,000	14,904	16,000	9,936
6	0.564	12,000	6,768	8,000	4,512
Total present value of cash inflows			1,06,756		1,12,272
Less : Total present value of cash outflows			1,00,000		1,00,000
Net Present value (NPV)			6,756		12,272

As net present value is grater in project II, it is preferable.

c. Excess present value index.

$$\frac{\text{Total Present value of Cash inf lows}}{\text{Total present value of cash outflows}} \times 100$$

$$\text{Project I} = \frac{1,08,756}{1,00,000} \times 100 = 107\%$$

$$\text{Project II} = \frac{1,12,272}{1,00,000} \times 100 = 112\%$$

24. Victoria Ltd. Is considering the purchase of one of the two machines. As the basis for selection, the following data was developed.

Original Cost	*Machine A (Rs)*	*Machine B (Rs.)*
Profit after tax	*25,565*	*25,565*
1	687	4687
2	1687	3687
3	2687	2687
4	3687	1687
5	4687	687
	13,435	13,435

The expected rate of return for the company is 16%. Both the machines have a life of 5 years and will not have any salvage value. The company is in the 40% tax bracket.

You are required to calculate NPV and PV index. Suggest the most profitable machine.

Year	*1*	*2*	*3*	*4*	*5*
PV factor at10%	0.862	0.743	0.641	0.552	0.476

Solution :

To ascertain present value, cash flows are to be taken in to account.

Cash flows = Profit after tax + depreciation
Depreciation = Profit after tax ÷ years
Machine A = 25,565 ÷ 5 Machine B = 25,565 ÷ 5
= 5,113 = 5,113

Calculation of Cash Inflows

Year		*Machine A*			*Machine B*	
	PAT	*Deprn*	*Cashinflows*	*PAT*	*Deprn*	*Cash inflows*
1	687	5,113	5,800	4687	5,113	9,800
2	1687	5,113	6,800	3687	5,113	8,800
3	2687	5,113	7,800	2687	5,113	7,800
4	3687	5,113	8,800	1687	5,113	6,800
5	4687	5,113	9,800	687	5,113	5,800

Calculation of Net Present Value

Year	*PV Factor at 10%*	*Machine A* *Cashinflows*	*PV of cash*	*Machine B* *Cashinflows inflows*	*PV of cashinflows*
1	0.862	5,800	5,000	9,800	8,448
2	0.743	6,800	5,052	8,800	6,538
3	0.641	7,800	5,000	7,800	5,000
4	0.552	8,800	4,858	6,800	3,754
5	0.476	9,800	4,665	5,800	2,761
TP value of cash inflows24,575				26,501	
Less : TP value of cash outflows			25,565		25,565
Net present value (NPV)- 990				936	

Present value Index

$$= \frac{\text{Total Present value of Cash inflows}}{\text{Total Prestn value of cash outflows}} \times 100$$

$$\text{Machine A} = \frac{24,575}{25,565} \times 100 = 96\%$$

$$\text{Machine B} = \frac{26,501}{25,565} \times 100 \times 100 = 104\%$$

The net present value is negative in the case of machine A. Machine B has a higher NPV of Rs. 936 index is also high for machine B. Hence machine B is recommended.

25. Bharath Ltd. has Rs. 2,00,000 to invest. The following proposals are under consideration. The cost of capital of the company is estimated to be 15%.

Project	*Initial outlay Rs.*	*Cash inflows Rs.*	*Life (years)*
A	1,00,000	25,000	10
B	70,000	20,000	8
C	30,000	6,000	20
D	50,000	15,000	10

Rank of projects on the basis of

a. Net Present value method

b. Profitability Index method

Solution :

P.V. of annuity of Re.1 received discounted at 5% is given below :

8 years - 4.487
10 years - 5.019
20 years - 6.259

Solution :

a. Net Present Value

Project (1)	*Cash inflows Rs. (2)*	*PV of annuity @15%*	*PV of cash inflows Rs. (4)*	*Invest-ment (5)*	*NPV Rs. (4-5)*	*Rank*	*Profit ability index %*	*Rank*
A	25,000	5.019	1,25,475	1,00,000	25,475	1	125.48	3
B	20,000	4.487	89,740	70,000	19,740	3	128.20	2

Contd...

Project (1)	*Cash inflows Rs. (2)*	*PV of annuity @15%*	*PV of cash inflows Rs. (4)*	*Invest-ment (5)*	*NPV Rs. (4-5)*	*Rank*	*Profit ability index %*	*Rank*
C	6,000	6.259	37,554	30,000	7,554	4	125.18	4
D	15,000	5.019	75,285	50,000	25,285	2	150.57	1

b. Profitability index

$$= \frac{\text{Total Present value of Cash inflows}}{\text{Total present value of cash outflows}} \times 100$$

Project A = × 100 = 125.48%

Project B = × 100 = 128.2%

Project C = × 100 = 125.18%

Project D = × 100 = ·150.57%

26. Lotus Ltd. is considering the purchase of a machine. Two alternative models are available relevant information is as follows.

	Machine X	*Machine Y*
Cost of the machine	3,00,000	5,00,000
Life time	4 years	5 years
Savings in scrap (Material)	45,000	50,000
Savings in wages	1,40,000	1,80,000
Supervision	10,000	15,000
Maintenance	6,000	10,000
Indirect material	4,000	5,000
Tax rate	50%	50%

Using discounted cash flow method, prepare a statement of profitability and recommend the profitable machine. At the prevailing rate of 12% the present value of Re.1 received annually for a. 4 years, Rs. 3.04, b. 5 years–Rs. 3.60

Solution :

Calculation of Cash Inflows

Particulars	*Machine X Rs.*	*Machine Y Rs.*
Savings in scrap	45,000	50,000
Savings in wages	1,40,000	1,80,000
Total savings (A)	1,85,000	2,30,000

Contd...

Particulars	*Machine X Rs.*	*Machine Y Rs.*
Additional cost :		
Supervision		
Maintenance	10,000	15,000
Indirect material	6,000	10,000
Depreciation	4,000	5,000
$\frac{3,00,000}{4}, \frac{5,00,000}{5}$	75,000	1,00,000
Total Additional Cost (B)	95,000	1,30,000
Profit before tax (A - B)	90,000	1,00,000
Less : Tax 50%	45,000	50,000
Profit after tax	45,000	50,000
Add: Depreciation	75,000	1,00,000
Annual Cash inflows	1,20,000	1,50,000

Calculation of Cash Inflows

Particulars	*Machine XRs.*	*Machine YRs.*
Annual Cash inflows	45,000	1,50,000
Present Value (4 years, 5 years)	3.04	3.60
Present value of cash inflows (45,000 × 3.04, 1,50,000 × 3.60)	3,64,800	5,40,000
Less : Present value of cash outflows	3,00,000	5,00,000
Net Present value (NPV)	64,800	40,000

Machine X is more profitable than machine Y.

27. Engine valves ltd. is considering building an assembly plant. The decision has been narrowed down to two possibilities. The company desires to choose the best plant at a level of operations of 10,000 gadgets a month. Both plants have an expected life of 10 years and are expected not to have any salvage value at the time of their retirement. The cost of capital is10%. Assuming a zero income tax rate, suggest what would be the desirable choice.

Cost of the Monthly Output of 10,000 Values

Particulars	Large plant Rs.	Small Plant Rs.
Initial Cost	30,00,000	22,93,500
Direct Labour:		
I Shift	15,00,000 p.a.	7,80,000 p.a.
II Shift		9,00,000 p.a
Overheads	2,40,000 p.a	2,10,000 p.a.

The present value of an ordinary annuity of Re. 1 for 10 years at 10% is 6.1446.

Solution :

Installation of large plant

Statements Showing Savings Per Annum

Direct labour for small plant (for both shifts 7,80,000+9,00,000)	16,80,000	
Less : Direct labour for large plant	15,00,000	
Savings on direct labour (Large plant)		1,80,000
Overheads costs for small plant	2,10,000	
Less : Overhead costs for large plant	2,40,000	
Additional Overhead costs (Large Plant)		-30,000
Net savings p.a. by using large plant		1,50,000

Present value for 10 years=1,50,000×6.1446 = 9,21,690
Cost of large plant = 30,00,000
Cost of small plant = 22,93,500
Additional cost of large plant = 7,06,500
Present value of savings from large plant = 9,21,690
Additional cost of large plant = 7,06,500
(Present value of cash inflows)
Net Present value (NPV) = 2,15,190

It is advisable to go in for the large plant as net present value is positive.

28. A company has an investment opportunity costing 40,000 with the following expected net cash flow, after tax but before depreciation.

Year	*Net cash flow Rs.*	*Year*	*Net Cash flow Rs.*
1	7,000	6	8,000
2	7,000	7	10,000
3	7,000	8	15,000
4	7,000	9	10,000
5	7,000	10	4,000

Using 10% are the rate of discount, find out the following.

1. Pay back period

2. Net present value

Solution :

1. Pay Back Period

Year	*Cash inflows Rs.*	*Cumulative Cashinflows Rs.*
1	7,000	7,000
2	7,000	14,000
3	7,000	21,000
4	7,000	28,000
5	7,000	35,000
6	8,000	43,000
7	10,000	53,000
8	15,000	68,000
9	10,000	78,000
10	4,000	82,000

Pay back period = 4 years and 8 months

40,000 - 35,000 = 5,000

43,000 – 35,000 = 8,000

$$\frac{5000}{8000} \times 12 \text{ months} = 8 \text{ months}$$

2. Net Present Value

Year	*Present value factor at 10%*	*Present value of cash inflows Rs.*	*Total present value of cash inflows Rs.*
1	0.909	7,000	6,363
2	0.826	7,000	5,782
3	0.751	7,000	5,257
4	0.683	7,000	4,781
5	0.621	7,000	4,347
6	0.564	8,000	4,512
7	0.513	10,000	5,130
8	0.467	15,000	7,005
9	0.424	10,000	4,240
10	0.386	4,000	1,544
Total Present value of cash inflows		48,961	
Less: Total present value of cash outflows			40,000
Net Present Value (NPV)			8,961

Net Present value is positive. Therefore, the project is recommended.

ACCOUNTING RATE OF RETURN

29. Calculate the average rate of return for projects A and B from the following.

	Project A	*Project B*
Investments	Rs. 20,000	Rs. 30,000
Expected Life	4 years	5 year

Projected Net income (After interest, depreciation and Taxes)

Years	*Project A Rs.*	*Project B Rs.*
1	2,000	3,000
2	1,500	3,000
3	1,500	2,000
4	1,000	1,000
5	-	1,000
	6,000	10,000

If the required rate of return is 12% which project should be undertaken ?

Solution :

$$\text{Average Profit} = \frac{\text{Total Profit}}{\text{Life of the Project}}$$

$$\text{Project A} = \frac{6000}{4\,\text{years}} = \text{Rs. } 1{,}500,$$

$$\text{Project B} = \frac{10000}{5\,\text{years}} = \text{Rs. } 2{,}000,$$

Investment in the Project : A = 20,000, B = 30,000

Accounting Rate of Return

$$= \frac{\text{Average Net Profit}}{\text{Original Investment}} \times 100$$

Project A = $\frac{1500}{20,000} \times 100$ = 7.5%, Project B = $\frac{2000}{30,000} \times 100$

= 6.67%

(or)

Accounting Rate of Return = × 100

Average Investment =

A = B =

= 10,000 = 15,000

Accounting rate of Return

A= × 100 = 15%, B = × 100 = 13.33%

30. A company is considering investment of Rs. 10,00,000 in a project. The following are the income forecasts, after depreciation and tax.

I year loss	Rs. 1,00,000
II year profit	Rs. 3,00,000
III year profit	Rs. 4,00,000
IV year profit	Rs. 2,00,000
V year profit	Rs. 2,00,000

Calculate the accounting rate of return.

a. On original investment method

b. On average investment method

Solution :

Average Profit =

$$\frac{3,00,000 + 4,00,00 + 2,00,000 + 2,00,000 - 1,00,000}{5\,\text{years}}$$

$$= \frac{10,00,000}{5\,\text{years}} = 2,00,000$$

a. on original investment method

$$= \frac{\text{Average Profit}}{\text{Original Investment}} \times 100$$

$$= \frac{2,00,000}{10,00,000} \times 100 = 20\%$$

b. On Average investment method

$$= \frac{\text{Average Profit}}{\text{Average Investment}} \times 100$$

$$\text{Average Investment} = \frac{10,00,000}{2} = 5,00,000$$

$$= \frac{2,00,000}{5,00,000} \times 100 = 40\%$$

31. A project requires on investment of Rs. 10,00,000. The plant and machinery required under the project will have a scrap value of Rs.80,000 at the end of its useful life of 5 years. The profit after tax and depreciation are estimated to be as follows.

Year	*Rs.*
1	50,000
2	75,000
3	1,25,000
4	1,30,000
5	80,000

Calculate the average annual rate of return.

Solution :

Average annual rate of return

$$= \frac{\text{Average Profit}}{\text{Average Investment}} \times 100$$

Average Profit =

$$\frac{50,000 + 75,000 + 1,25,000 + 1,30,000 + 80,000}{5 \text{ years}} = 92,000$$

$$\text{Average Investment} = \frac{10,00,000 + 80,000}{2} = 5,40,000$$

Average annual Rate of return

$$= \frac{92,000}{5,40,000} \times 100 = 17\%$$

32. A company has two alternative proposals. The details are

Particulars	*Proposal I* *Automatic Machine*	*Proposal II* *Ordinary Machine*
Cost of the machine	Rs. 2,20,000	Rs.60,000
Estimated life	5½ years	8 years
Estimated sales p.a.	Rs. 1,50,000	Rs.1,50,000
Costs :		
Material	50,000	50,000
Labour	12,000	60,000
Variable overheads	24,000	20,000

Compute the profitability of the proposals under the return on investment method.

Solution :

Profitability Statement

Particulars	*Proposal I* *Automatic Machine*	*Proposal II* *Ordinary Machine*
Cost of the machine	Rs. 2,20,000	Rs.60,000
Life of the Machine	5½ years	8 years
Estimated sales (A)	Rs. 1,50,000	Rs.1,50,000
Costs :		
Material	50,000	50,000
Labour	12,000	60,000
Variable overheads	24,000	20,000
Depreciation	40,000	7,500
Total Cost (B)	1,26,000	1,37,500
Profit (A-B)	24,000	12,500

$$\text{Return on investment} = \frac{\text{Average Profit}}{\text{Original Investment}} \times 100$$

$$\text{Automatic Machine} = \frac{24,000}{2,20,000} \times 100 = 10.9\%$$

$$\text{Ordinary Machine} = \frac{12,500}{60,000} \times 100 = 20.8\%$$

Automatic machine is more profitable than the ordinary machine.

33. The Directors of A Ltd Co consider a proposal to invest a sum of Rs.1,00,000 on a plant that has an expected life of 5 years which at the end has no residual value.

The expected annual incomes during the life of the plant are:

	Rs.
I year	30,000
II year	40,000
III year	40,000
IV year	30,000
V year	20,000
	1,60,000

Money is available at on interest of 10% p.a. calculate rate of return and advise the directors of the company.

Solution :

$$\text{Rate of Return} = \frac{\text{Average Pr ofit}}{\text{Original Investment}} \times 100$$

$$\text{Average Profit} = \frac{1,60,000}{5} = 32,000$$

$$= \frac{32,000}{1,00,000} \times 100 = 32\%$$

34. The following particulars relate to two machine producing identical products.

	Machine A	*Machine B*
Original Cost	Rs. 1,00,000	Rs. 1,50,000
Working life	5 years	5 years
Profit before depreciation	Rs.	Rs.
I year	30,000	40,000
II year	15,000	45,000
III year	40,000	50,000

Contd...

	Machine A	Machine B
IV year	40,000	24,000
V year	35,000	71,000
Tax rate	50%	50%

a. Calculate return on investments.

b. Calculate Average rate o return assuming that machines A and B have scrap values of Rs.10,000 and Rs.20,000 respectively at the end of 5th year.

Solution :

$$\text{Depreciation} = \frac{\text{Cost} - \text{Scrap Value}}{\text{Life of the machin}}$$

$$\text{Machine A} = \frac{1,00,000 - 10,000}{5} = \text{Rs.}18,000$$

$$\text{Machine B} = \frac{1,50,000 - 20,000}{5} = \text{Rs. } 20,000$$

Calculation of Profit-Machine A

Year	Profit before deprn and tax	Deprn Rs.	Profit after deprn Rs.	Tax at 50% Rs.	Profit after tax Rs.
1	30,000	18,000	12,000	6,000	6,000
2	15,000	18,000	-3,000	-	-3,000
3	40,000	18,000	22,000	11,000	11,000
4	40,000	18,000	22,000	11,000	11,000
5	35,000	18,000	17,000	8,500	8,500
		Total Profit			33,500

$$\text{Average annual profit} = \frac{33,500}{5} = \text{Rs.}6,700$$

Calculation of profit – Machine B

Year	Profit before deprn and tax	Deprn Rs.	Profit after deprn Rs.	Tax at 50% Rs.	Profit after tax Rs.
1	40,000	26,000	14,000	7,000	7,000
2	45,000	26,000	19,000	9,500	9,500
3	50,000	26,000	24,000	12,000	12,000
4	24,000	26,000	-2,000	-	-2,000
5	71,000	26,000	45,000	22,500	22,500
		Total Profit			49,000

$$\text{Average Annual Profit} = \frac{49{,}000}{5} = 9{,}800$$

$$\text{Return on investment} = \frac{\text{Average Annual Profit}}{\text{Original Investment}} \times 100$$

$$\text{Machine A} = \frac{6{,}700}{1{,}00{,}000} \times 100 = 6.7\%$$

$$\text{Machine B} = \frac{9{,}800}{1{,}50{,}000} \times 100 = 6.53\%$$

Return on average investment

$$= \frac{\text{Average Annual Profit}}{\text{Average Investment}} \times 100$$

Average investment

$$= \frac{\text{Opening investment} + \text{Closing Investment}}{2}$$

$$\text{Machine A} = \frac{1{,}00{,}000 + 10{,}000}{2} = \text{Rs. } 55{,}000$$

$$\text{Machine B} = \frac{1{,}50{,}000 + 20{,}000}{2} = \text{Rs. } 85{,}000$$

Return on average investment

$$\text{Machine A} = \frac{6{,}700}{55{,}000} \times 100 = 12.18\%$$

$$\text{Machine B} = \frac{9{,}800}{85{,}000} \times 100 = 11.52\%$$

35. Beta Ltd. is considering the purchase of a new machine to replace a machine which has been in operation in the factory for the last 5 years.

Ignoring interest but considering tax at 50% of net earnings, suggest which of the two alternatives should be preferred. The following are the details.

	Old Machine	New Machine
Purchase price	Rs. 40,000	Rs.60,000
Estimated life of machine	10 years	10 years
Machine running hours p.a.	2,000	2,000
Units per hour	24	36
Wages per running hour	3	5.25
Power p.a.	2,000	4,500
Consumable stores p.a.	6,000	7,500
All other charges p.a.	8,000	9,000
Material cost per unit	0.50	0.50
Selling price per unit	1.25	1.25

You may assume that the above information regarding sales and cost of sales will hold good through out the economic life of each of the machines. Depreciation has to be charged according to straight line method. Calculate accounting rate of return.

Solution :

Profitability Statement

Particulars	Old Machine		New Machine	
Cost of the machine (Rs)		40,000		60,000
Life of Machine (yrs)		10		10
Out put (units)	2000 × 24	48,000	2000 × 36	72,000
Sales value (Rs)		60,000		90,000
Less: Cost of Sales:				
Direct material (48,000 × 0.50, 72,000 × 0.50)	24,000		36,000	
Wages (2,000 × 3, 2000 × 5.25)	6,000		10,500	
Power	2,000		4,500	
Consumable Stores	6,000		7, 500	
Other charges	8,000		9,000	
Depreciation $\frac{40,000}{10\,year}, \frac{60,000}{10\,yrs}$	4,000		6,000	
		50,000		73,500
Profit before tax		10,000		16,500
Less : Tax 50%		5,000		8,250
Profit After tax		5,000		8,250

$$\text{Accounting Rate of Return} = \frac{\text{Average Net Profit}}{\text{Original Investment}} \times 100$$

$$\text{Old Machine} = \frac{5,000}{40,000} \times 100 = 12.5\ \%$$

$$\text{New Machine} = \frac{8,250}{60,000} \times 100 = 13.75\ \%$$

(or)

$$\frac{\text{Average Net profit}}{\text{Average Investment}} \times 100$$

$$\text{Old Machine}\ \frac{5,000}{20,000} = \times 100 = 25\ \%$$

$$\text{New Machine} = \frac{8,250}{30,000} \times 100 = 27.50\ \%$$

Thus, replacement of the old machinery by a new machine a plant.

36.

	Machine X	*Machine Y*
Estimated life	3 years	3 years
Capital Cost	Rs. 90,000	Rs.90,000
Earnings after tax		
1 year	40,000	20,000
2 year	50,000	70,000
3 year	40,000	50,000

The company follows the straight line method of depreciation. The estimation salvage value of both the types of machines is zero.

Show the most profitable investment based on

1. Pay back period.
2. Accounting Rate of Return and

3. Net present value method using 10% cost of capital.

Solution :

1. Pay back period method

Year	*Machine X*		*Machine Y*	
	Cash inflows	*Cumulative cash inflows*	*Cash inflows*	*Cumulative cash inflows*
1	40,000	40,000	20,000	20,000
2	50,000	90,000	70,000	90,000
3	40,000	1,30,000	50,000	1,40,000

Pay back period = 2 years for X and Y.

2. Accounting Rate of Return

$$\text{On original Method} = \frac{\text{Average Profit}}{\text{Original Investment}} \times 100$$

$$\text{On average investment} = \frac{\text{Average Profit}}{\text{Average Investment}} \times 100$$

$$\text{Average Profit X} = \frac{40,000 + 50,000 + 40,000}{3\,\text{years}} = 43,333$$

$$\text{Y} = \frac{20,000 + 70,000 + 50,000}{3\,\text{years}} = 46,667$$

Accounting Rate of Return :

$$\text{X} = \frac{43,333}{90,000} \times 100 = 48\%$$

$$\text{Y} = \frac{46,667}{90,000} \times 100 = 52\%$$

3. Net Present Value Method

$$\text{Depreciation X} = \frac{90,000}{3\,\text{years}} = 30,000, \text{Y} = \frac{90,000}{3\,\text{years}} = 30,000$$

Year	PV	Machine X				Machine Y			
	Factor	PAT	Deprn	Cash	Present	PAT	Deprn	Cash	Present
1	0.909	40,000	30,000	70,000	63,630	20,000	30,000	50,000	45,450
2	0.826	50,000	30,000	80,000	66,080	70,000	30,000	1,00,000	82,600
3	0.751	40,000	30,000	70,000	52,570	50,000	30,000	80,000	60,080
Total Present value of cash inflows					1,82,280				1,88,130
Less : Total value of cash outflows					90,000				90,000
Net Present value (NPV)					92,280				98,130

Machine Y is preferable because it has a higher amount of Net present value.

37. A Limited company is considering investing in a project requiring a capital outlay of Rs. 2,00,000. Forecast of annual income after depreciation but before tax is as follows:

Year	Rs.
1	1,00,000
2	1,00,000
3	80,000
4	80,000
5	40,000

Depreciation may be taken as 20% on original cost and taxation at 50% of net income, calculate.

a. Pay back method
b. Rate of return on original investment
c. Rate of return on average investment
d. Discounted cash flow method taking cost of capital at 10%
e. Excess present value Index

Solution :

$$\text{Depreciation} = \frac{2,00,000}{5\,\text{years}} = 40,000$$

a. Pay back method

Year	Profit	Tax at 50%	PAT	Deprn	Cash inflows	Cumulative cash inflows
1	1,00,000	50,000	50,000	40,000	90,000	90,000
2	1,00,000	50,000	50,000	40,000	90,000	1,80,000
3	80,000	40,000	40,000	40,000	80,000	2,60,000
4	80,000	40,000	40,000	40,000	80,000	3,40,000
5	40,000	20,000	20,000	40,000	60,000	4,00,000

Pay back period = 2 years and 3 months.

2,00,000 – 1,80,000 = 20,000

2,60,000 – 1,80,000 = 80,000

20,000/80,000 × 12 months = 3 months

b. Rate of Return on original investment method

Year	Net profit after tax and depreciation (Rs)
1	50,000
2	50,000
3	40,000
4	40,000
5	20,000
Total	2,00,000

$$\text{Average Annual Profit} = \frac{2,00,000}{5\,\text{years}} = 40,000$$

$$\text{Rate of Return} = \frac{40,000}{2,00,000} \times 100 = 20\%$$

c. Rate of Return on average Investment method

$$= \frac{40,000}{1,00,000} \times 100 = 40\%$$

d. Discounted cash flow method

Year	PV factor at 10%	Cash inflows	Present value of cash inflows Rs.
1	0.909	90,000	81,810
2	0.826	90,000	74,340
3	0.751	80,000	60,080

Contd...

Year	PV factor at 10%	Cash inflows	Present value of cash inflows Rs.
4	0.683	80,000	54,640
5	0.621	60,000	37,260
Total Present value of cash inflows			3,08,130
Less : Total Present value of cash outflows			2,00,000
Net Present value (NPV)			1,08,130

e. Excess Present value Index

$$= \frac{\text{Total Present value of cash inflows}}{\text{Total Present value of cash outflows}} \times 100$$

$$= \frac{3,08,130}{2,00,000} \times 100 = 154\%$$

INTERNAL RATE OF RETURN (IRR)

38. Initial outlay Rs.50,000
    Life of the Asset 5 years
    Estimated cash flow Rs. 12,500

Calculate Internal rate of return

Solution :

$$\text{Present value factor} = \frac{\text{Initial Investment}}{\text{annual cash inflow}}$$

$$= \frac{50,000}{12,500} = 4$$

The present value factor is to be located in the present value Annuity table in the column of 5 years (life of the assets). The figure 3.9927 (neares to 4) is found in the row of 8% Hence internal rate of return is 8%.

39. Initial Investment Rs. 60,000
    Life of the Asset 4 years
    Estimated net annual cash flows
    I year Rs. 15,000
    II year Rs. 20,000
    III year Rs. 30,000
    IV year Rs. 20,000

Calculate internal rate of return.

Note: The following table gives the present value of Re.1 due in the number of years.

Year	*P.V. Factor at 10%*	*P.V. Factor at 12%*	*P.V. Factor at 14%*	*P.V. factor at 15%*
1	0.909	0.892	0.877	0.869
2	0.826	0.797	0.769	0.756
3	0.751	0.711	0.674	0.657
4	0.683	0.635	0.592	0.571

Solution :

Cash Flow Table at Discount Rates of 10%, 12% 14% and 15%

Year	*Annual cash inflow*	*P.V.F 10%*	*PV. Rs.*	*P.V.F. 12%*	*P.V. Rs.*	*P.V.F. 14%*	*P.V. Rs.*	*P.V.F. 15%*	*P.V. Rs.*
1	15,000	0.909	13,635	0.892	13,380	0.877	13,155	0.869	13,035
2	20,000	0.826	16,520	0.797	15,940	0.769	15,380	0.756	15,120
3	30,000	0.751	22,530	0.711	21,330	0.674	20,220	0.657	19,710
4	20,000	0.683	13,660	0.635	12,700	0.592	11,840	0.571	11,420
Total P.V. of Cash inflows			66,345		63,350		60,595		59,285

At 14% total present value = 60,595

At 15% total present value = 59,285

$$15\% - 14\% = 1\% = 1{,}310$$

$$60{,}595 - 60{,}000 = 595$$

$$\frac{595}{1{,}310} \times 1\% = 0.45\%$$

$$IRR = 14\% + 0.45\% = 14.45\%$$

40. A machine costing Rs.11,00,000 has a life of 10 years at the end of which its scrap value is likely to be Rs.1,00,000. The firms cut off rate is 12%. The machine is expected to yield an annual profit after tax of Rs.1,00,000. Depreciation is charged on straight line basis for tax purposes. At 12% P.V. of rupee 1 received annually for 10 years is 5.650 and

the value of one rupee received at the end of the 10th year is 0.322. Calculate NPV.

Solution :

Calculation of Net Present Value

	Rs.
Annual Profit after tax	1,00,000
Add: Depreciation 11,00,000–1,00,00010,00,000 ÷ 10 years	1,00,000
Annual cash inflows	2,00,000
Present value of cash inflows for 10 years at 12% (2,00,000 × 5.650)	11,30,000
Add: Salvage value at the end of 10th year (1,00,000 × 0.322)	32,200
Total present value of cash inflows	11,62,200
Less : Investment	11,00,000
Net Present Value (NPV)	62,200

41. An investor who must have a minimum rate of return of 12% p.a. has two projects in view, both requiring initial outlay of Rs. 30,000. Project A given an annual net income of Rs. 6,000 with a salvage value of Rs.10,000 at the end of 10 years. Project B given an annual net income of Rs. 5,000 with a salvage value of Rs.2,000 at the end of 10 years. Which project should be prefer ? (PV of Re.1 at 12% received annually for 10 years = 5.65 and at the end of 10th year = 0.322).

Solution :

Calculation of Net Present Value

Particulars	*Project A*	*Project B*
Annual profit after tax	6,000	5,000
Add: Depreciation (30,000 – 10,000, 30,000 – 200020,000 ÷ 10 years) 28000 ÷10	2,000	2,800
Annual Cash inflows	8,000	7,800
P.V. of cash inflows for 10 years at 12% (8,000 × 5.65, 7800 × 5.65)	45,200	44,070
Add: Salvage value (10,000 × 0.322, 2000 × 0.322)	3,220	644

Contd...

Particulars	*Project A*	*Project B*
Total P.V. of cash inflows	48,420	44,714
Less : Investment	30,000	30,000
Net Present Value (NPV)	18,420	14,714

42. National steel co., is considering to invest in a project which cost Rs.2,50,000 and will require an increase in the level of inventories and receivables (working capital) of Rs. 1,25,000 over its life. The project will generate additional sales of Rs. 2,50,000 and will require additional expenses of Rs. 75,000 every year. The project has 5 years life. The firms cost of capital is 10% and is in the tax bracket of 50%.

    Assuming straight line method of depreciation should the project be accepted?

    Present value of an annuity of Re.1 at 10% for 5 years is 6.105.

Solution :

		Rs.
I. Total cash outflows		
Cost of the new project	=	2,50,000
Add: Additional working capital	=	1,25,000
Total Cash outflows	=	3,75,000
II. Annual Cash inflows:		
Additional sales revenue	=	2,50,000
Less : Additional Expenses	=	75,000
		1,75,000
Less : Depreciation 2,50,000 ÷ 5 years		50,000
Profit before tax (PBT)		1,25,000
Less : Tax at 50%		62,500
Profit after tax (PAT)		62,500
Add: Depreciation		50,000
Annual Cash inflows		1,12,500
P.V. of cash inflows for 5 years (1,12,500 × 6.105)		6,86,813
Less : Net cash outflows		3,75,000
Net Present value (NPV)		3,11,813

Comment: Since the NPV is positive, the project should be accepted.

43. Apple Industries Ltd., is considering two mutually exclusive proposals A and B.

Proposals A: Proposal A will cost Rs. 1,40,000 with no salvage value and will require an increase in the level of inventories and receivables (working capital) Rs. 60,000 over its life. The project will generate additional sales of Rs. 1,30,000 and will require cash expenses of Rs. 40,000 in each of its 5 year life. It will be depreciated on straight line basis.

The earnings before depreciation and tax and as follows.

Year	1	2	3	4	5
Earnings (Rs)	70,000	76,000	80,000	90,000	92,000

The company's cost of capital is 10% and tax rate is 35%.

Which project is acceptable under NPV method ?

Assume working capital will realize at the end of the 5th year.

Note : P.V of annuity of Re.1 at the end of 5 years is 3,791.
P.V. of Re.1 at 14% at the end of 5th year is 0.621.

Solution :

Proposal: A

1. Total Cash outflows

Cost of the project	=	Rs. 1,40,000
Add: Working capital required	=	60,000
Total Cash outflows		2,00,000

2. Cash inflows

Additional Sales	Rs. 1,30,000
Less : Cash Expenses	40,000
	90,000
Less: Depreciation (1,40,000 ÷ 5 yrs)	28,000
Profit before tax	62,000

Less : Tax at 35%	21,700
Profit After Tax	40,300
Add: Depreciation	28,000
Annual Cash inflows	68,300

3. Calculation of NPV

P.V. of cash inflows for 5yrs (68,300 × 3.791)	=	2,58,925
Add : Working Capital	=	37,260
(60,000 × 0.621)	=	2,96,185
Less : Total Cash outflows	=	2,00,000
Net Present Value	=	96,185

Proposal : B

Year	*Earnings Rs.*	*deprn Rs.*	*earnings After Deprn Rs.*	*Tax 35% Rs.*	*EAT Rs.*	*Cash inflows Rs.*	*P.V. Factor at 10%*	*P.V. of Cash inflows*
1	70,000	40,000	30,000	10,500	19,500	59,500	0.909	54,086
2	76,000	40,000	36,000	12,600	23,400	63,400	0.826	52,368
3	80,000	40,000	40,000	14,000	26,000	66,000	0.751	49,566
4	90,000	40,000	50,000	17,500	32,500	72,500	0.683	49,518
5	92,000	40,000	52,000	18,200	33,800	73,800	0.621	45,830

Total Present Value of cash inflows2,51,368
Less: total Present Value of cash outflows2,00,000
Net Present Value (NPV)51,368

Comment : Proposal A has higher NPV that proposal B. Hence Proposal B is suggested.

44. Nirmala Corporation purchased a machine 5 years back at a cost of Rs. 75,000. The machine had an expected life of 15 years at the time of purchase and zero salvage value at the end of 15 years. It is being depreciated on a straight line method and has a book value of Rs. 50,000 at present. The purchase manager reports that he can buy a new machine for Rs. 1,50,000 which has 10 year life. The existing sales are Rs. 1,00,000 and are expected to go

up by Rs. 10,000 on account of purchase of a new machine. Further, it will reduce the cash operating cost from Rs. 70,000 to Rs. 50,000. The current market value of old machine is Rs. 10,000. The firm's cost of capital is 10% and the tax rate is 50%.

Calculate net cash out flows of the new project and net cash inflows.

Solution :

1. Net Cash outflows

Cost of new machine	1,50,000
Less: Cash inflow from the sale of old machine (Current market value)	10,000
	1,40,000
Less : Tax saving on account of loss on sale (Book value – sale value) (50,000 – 10,000 = 40,000 × 50/100)	20,000
Net Cash outflow	1,20,000

2. Net cash Outflows

Particulars	*Old Machine*	*New Machine*
Sales	1,00,000	1,10,000
Less : Cash operating cost	70,000	50,000
	30,000	60,000
Less : Depreciation		
$\frac{75,000-0}{15\,\text{year}}, \frac{1,50,000-0}{15\,\text{year}}$	5,000	15,000
Profit before tax	25,000	45,000
Less : Tax at 50%	12,500	22,500
Profit after tax	12,500	22,500
Add: Depreciation	5,000	15,000
Cash inflows	17,500	37,500

Comment: If the new machine is purchased there will be an incremental cash inflow of Rs. 20,000 (37,500 - 17,500). Hence, the purchase of a new machine is suggested.

45. Sun glas Ltd. is contemplating to replace one of its bottling machine with a new and more efficient machine. The old machine cost Rs. 5,00,000 and has a useful life of 10 years and zero salvage value at the end of 10th year. The machine was bought 5 years ago. If it is sold now, the company would get Rs. 3,00,000.

    The new machine cost Rs.10,00,000 and has a salvage value of Rs. 1,00,000 at the end of the 5th year.

    The new machine will have a greater capacity and annual sales are expected to increase from Rs. 10,00,000 to Rs. 12,00,000. Operating efficiency of new machine will also produce savings of Rs. 2,00,000 a year. Straight line method of depreciation is followed. The cost of capital is 8% and 30% tax rate is applicable.

    Should the company replace the old machine?

Note : P.V. annuity Re.1 at 8% for 5 years is 3.993
P.V. of Re.1 at 8% for 5 years is 0.681

Solution :

1. Net Cash outflows

	Rs.
Cost of New Machine	10,00,000
Less: Cash inflow from sale of old machine	3,00,000
Add: Tax on profit on sale	7,00,000
(Book value- Sale Value	
2,50,000 – 3,00,000 = 50,000 × 30/100)	15,000
	7,15,000

Calculation of Book Value

Depreciation = 5,00,000 ÷ 10 years = 50,000

Depreciation for 5 years = 50,000 × 5 = 2,50,000

Book Value = Cost - Depreciation

= 5,00,000 – 2,50,000 = 2,50,000

2. Net Cash inflows

Increase in Sale	2,00,000
Add : Income due to increase in operating Efficiency	2,00,000
	4,00,000

Less: Incremental Depreciation

New Machine

$$10,00,000 - 1,00,000 = \frac{9,00,000}{5} = 1,80,000$$

Old machine 5,00,000 ÷ 10	50,000
	1,30,000
Profit before tax	2,70,000
Less: Tax at 30%	81,000
Profit after tax	1,89,000
Add: Depreciation	1,30,000
Annual Cash inflows	3,19,000

3. Calculation of NPV

P.V. of cash inflows for 5 years (3,19,000 × 3.993)	12,73,767
Add : Salvage value at the end of 5 years (1,00,000 × 0.681)	68,100
Total P.V. of cash inflows	13,41,867
Less: Total P.V. of cash outflows	7,15,000
Net Present value (NPV)	6,26,867

Since NPV is positive, the company can replace the old machine.

Chapter 6

FINANCIAL PLANNING AND FORECASTING

Meaning of Financial Planning

We have explained that the funds requirement decision and the financing decision are two the major areas of financial decision making. Funds requirements decision is concerned with the estimation of the total funds or capital requirements for the business enterprise while the financing decision is concerned with the sources from which the funds are to be raised.

Financial planning, therefore includes

i. Estimation of the amount of capital to be raised.
ii. Determining the form and proportionate amount of securities.
iii. Laying down the policies as to the administration of the financial plan.

Meaning of Financial plan

Financial planning result in the formulation of the financial plan. It is primarily a statement estimating the amount of capital and determining its composition. It states,

1. The quantum of finance
2. The patterns of financing
3. The policies to be pursued for the floatation of various corporate securities.

Principles Governing A Financial Plan

The financial plan should be prepared keeping in view the following principles.

1. Simplicity
2. Long term view
3. Far sight
4. Optimum use
5. Contingencies
6. Flexibility
7. Liquidity
8. Economy

Estimating Capital Requirements

The capital requirements of a business enterprise can broadly be classified into two main categories, they are

a. Fixed capital requirements and
b. Working capital requirements

A. Fixed Capital Requirements

Meaning

Fixed capital means the capital which is meant for meeting the permanent or long term needs of the business. In other words, fixed capital is required for the acquisition of those assets that are to be used over a long period.

Fixed capital is required for the acquisition of the following assets

1. Tangible assets such as land, buildings, plant and machinery, furniture and fixture etc.
2. Intangible assets such as goodwill, patents, copy rights, promotion cost etc.

Assessment of Fixed Capital Requirements

The assessment of fixed capital requirements for a business can be made by preparing a list of the fixed assets needed by the business. Having compiled a list of the fixed assets required for

1. Banking and custody
2. Credit and collection

3. Investments
4. Insurance

Financial Forecasting

Meaning

The term "Forecasting" refers to the formal process of predicting future events which are going to affect significantly the functioning of an enterprise. Financial forecasting therefore, implies the technique of determining in advance the requirement and utilization of funds for a future period. It is a technique of systematic presentation of data in the form of financial statements ratios etc. It uses the following techniques such as

i. Percentage of sales method
ii. Simple regression method
iii. Multiple regression method

Uses or Utility

Financial forecasting has immense utility for a business organization on accounts of the following reasons.

i. It generates useful information for financial decision making.
ii. It provides significant information for successful financial planning.
iii. It facilitates the firms to plan for its growth and the financial needs.
iv. It functions as a contract device by providing a standard of financial performance for the future.
v. It enables the firm to make optimal utilization of its funds.
vi. It makes the firm to adopt appropriate financial policies.

Preparation of Iinancial Statement

1. Proforma Income statement
2. Proforma Balance Sheet

3. Proforma fund flow statement
4. Cash Budget

Financial Management Science or Art

Financial management is both a science and an art. Of course, it is neither a pure science like physics nor an art like painting. It lies some where in between it is a science because it consists of certain basic principles and procedures based on various theories propounded by financial experts, viz., cost of capital theories, capital structure theories etc. It also takes the help of various statistical techniques, econometric models, computer technology, etc. for taking financial decisions like budgeting decision, investment decision, capital structure decisions etc. As a result it will be appropriate to say that financial management is an applied science.

Objectives of Financial Planning

The objectives of financial planning are

1. To determine the financial resources required for meeting fixed capital and working capital needs.
2. To forecast the amount of internal generation of funds as well as the external resources.
3. To decide an appropriate mix of debt and equity which will maximize shareholders wealth.
4. To develop plans to secure necessary funds from external sources at the minimum possible cost.
5. To formulate programmes to provide the most effective cost volume profit relationships.
6. To establish and maintain a system of financial control to monitor the allocation and utilisation of funds.
7. To analyse the financial results and report to the top management.

Factors Influencing Financial Planning

Financial planning is a crucial exercise. It has significant impact on the operations of a company. The following factors are to be carefully considered in financial planning.

1. Nature of the industry.
2. General Economic Environment.
3. Plans for Expansion and Diversification
4. Sources of funds and their costs
5. Reputation of the firm
6. Government facilities

Estimating Capital Requirement

Finance is required for meeting long term as well as short term needs of business. Hence, financial planning involves an estimation of both fixed capital and working capital requirements.

Fixed Capital

Fixed capital is the capital required for meeting the permanent long term needs of the business. More specifically, fixed capital is necessary for the following purposes.

1. Purchase of fixed assets like buildings, plant and machinery, furniture etc.
2. Acquisition of intangible assets like goodwill, patents and copyrights.
3. Meeting promotion expenses.
4. Meeting permanent working capital needs.

Determination of Fixed Capital

1. Nature of the business
2. Size of the business
3. Diversity of production lines.
4. Methods of production

Working Capital

Working capital refers to capital which is required for financing day to day operations of the company. Working capital is needed for the following purposes.

1. To purchase raw materials, spares and components and parts.
2. To pay wages and salaries
3. To incur day to day expenses
4. To meet selling costs such as advertising, packing
5. To provide credit facilities to customers,
6. To maintain inventory of raw materials.

Determinants of Working Capital

The factors which determine working capital requirements of a business are

1. Nature of the business
2. Size of the business
3. Time taken for manufacture
4. Seasonal fluctuations in sales
5. Fluctuations in supply of raw materials.
6. Speed of Turnover
7. Terms of sales
8. Terms of purchase
9. Labour intensive Vs. Capital intensive industries
10. Growth and Expansion of business

Capitalisation

Capitalization is a crucial element in financial planning. In common parlance, capitalisation signifies the total amount of capital employed in business. However, experts on financial management have defined the term in many ways. These definitions fall into two major categories.

Broad Interpretation

According to this interpretation, capitalization is the same as financial planning. It refers to the amount of capital to be raised, the type and proportion of securities to be issued and the administration of capital.

Narrow Interpretation

In a narrow sense, capitalization refers only to the amount of long term funds required by a company. The type and proportion of securities are outside the purview of capitalization. The narrow interpretation is more specific and widely accepted. According to Gerstenberg, "Capitalization comprises ownership capital which includes capital stocks and surplus in whatever form it may appear and borrowed capital which consists of bonds or similar evidence of long term debt".

Thus capitalization includes the following

1. Equity share capital
2. Preference share capital
3. Reserves and Surplus
4. Debentures/Bonds
5. Other long term loans

Capital and Capitalization

Capital and capitalization mean different things. capital in a broad sense, refers to the total investment in tangible assets, intangible assets and cash. It represents the total wealth of the company.

Capital also refers to net capital. When used in this sense, capital refers to the excess of assets over liabilities (capital = Assets – liabilities)

Capitalization, on the other hand, refers to the total amount of long term funds. It includes share capital, reserves and surplus (or retained earnings), debentures (or bonds) and long term loans. The term 'capitalization' is used only in relation to companies.

Theories of Capitalization

There are two important approaches to determine the amount of capitalization.

1. *The cost Theory of capitalization:* This theory considers cost as the basis of capitalization. According to this

theory, capitalization of a new company is the total amount required to meet the following costs.

a. Cost of fixed assets like land, building, plant etc.
b. Permanent working capital required for the continuous operations of the company.
c. Cost of establishing the business.
d. Expenses on promotion.

Example

Capitalization of a new company	*Rs. in Crores*
Cost of fixed assets	60.00
Permanent working capital	5.00
Cost of establishing the business	1.00
Expenses on promotion	0.50
Total capitalization	66.50

MERITS

1. The cost theory is very simple
2. The cost theory helps to calculate the capital required a new business. It enables the promoters to know the amount of finance to be raised.

DEMERITS

But this theory is not satisfactory on account of the following reasons.

1. The capitalization is based on costs. It does not consider the earnings capacity of the business. The capitalization will remain the same irrespective of the earning capacity of the business.
2. Some of the assets may remain idle or become obsolete. Naturally, the earning capacity will be affected. But still, the capitalization will remain high, as it is based on the cost of assets.

EARNINGS THEORY OF CAPITALIZATION

The worth of a company depends on its earning capacity and not on the capital raised. Hence the earnings theory rightly recognizes earnings as the basis for the capitalization of the company.

Capitalization of a company is estimated on the basis of the earnings and the expected rate of return. For example, suppose the estimated earnings of A Ltd. Is Rs. 1 crore per annum and the fair rate of return expected is 10%. The capitalization of the company is :

For a return of Rs. 10, capitalization required = Rs. 100

Fro earnings Rs. 1 Crore, capitalization required = 1 crore x = Rs.10 crores.

The amount of capitalization is Rs. 10 crores

The fair rate of return depends on the nature and conditions of the industry, promoter's expectations, normal earning capacity etc.

Merits

1. The earnings theory is quite logical. It has the merit of valuing a company on the basis of its earning capacity. Capitalization represents the true worth of the company.
2. The capitalization arrived at on the basis of earnings can be used as a standard for comparison.

Demerits

1. Estimation of further earnings is not easy. If the earnings are not estimated correctly, the capitalization amount would be misleading.
2. It short, the cost theory of capitalization may be adopted by new companies (particularly when earnings can not be estimated). On the other hand,; earnings theory may be adopted by companies which can estimate their earnings without much difficulty.

Actual Capitalization vs. Standard Capitalization

Actual capitalization of a company is the sum total of share capital, reserves and surplus, debentures, bonds and other long term loans.

Standard or proper capitalization refer the amount of capitalization calculated on the basis of cost or earnings. The actual capitalization may be compared with the standard capitalization.

If actual capitalization is more than the standard, the company is said to be over capitalized and vice versa.

Over Capitalization

Over capitalization refers to the situation where the actual capitalization is more than the proper capitalization. In other words actual capitalization is higher than that is warranted by its earnings.

Example

Earnings of the Company	Rs. 12,00,000 P.a
Expected return (or) Capitalization rate	12 % p.a
Proper capitalization = 12,00,000 x 100/12	Rs. 1 Crore
Actual capitalization of the company	Rs. 2 Crores

It is evident that capitalization required to earn Rs. 12 lakhs is only Rs. 1 crore. But the actual capitalization is Rs. 2 crores. Hence, the company is over capitalized.

An over capitalized company is not able to earn a fair return on its capitalization. In the above example, the actual capitalization is Rs.2 crores and the earnings are Rs.12 lakhs.

The actual rate of return is 12,00,000/2,00,00,000 × 100 = 6% and it is quite low.

In the words of Gilbert, "when a company has consistently been unable to earn the prevailing rate of return on its outstanding securities (capitalization) it is said to be over capitablised".

Reasons for Over Capitalization

The reasons for over capitalization are

1. *Raising of excess funds:* The company may raise more funds than necessary. As a result, the funds may remain idle, leading to a lower overall return on investment.

2. *Excessive interest:* If the borrowings are large and the rate of interest is high, large part of the earnings has to be paid out as interest. The earnings of shareholders will be adversely affected and the rate of dividend will decline.
3. *Excess payment for fixed assets:* The promoters might have paid unreasonable amounts for goodwill and fixed assets. In other words, price paid for the assets is much higher than their real worth. The earning is low whereas the capitalization is high.
4. *Purchase of assets during boom period:* If a company purchases the assets during a boom period, price paid for them is naturally high. When recession sets in the value of assets decline. Their earning capacity is also affected. But the assets will continue to appear in the books at higher values. The result is over capitalization.
5. *Inadequate provision for depreciation:* If a company does not make adequate provision for depreciation and replacement of assets, profit will be over stated. In course of time, the assets will become obsolete and their earning capacity will decline. The earnings will below. But, book value of assets and capitalization will be disproportionately high, compared to the earnings.
6. *Higher rates of taxation:* Higher tax rates take away a large portion of profits. The company may not have adequate profits to provide for depreciation and replacement of assets.
7. *Under estimation of capitalization rate:* Capitalization rate or the rate of expected return is an important determinant of capitalization. For example suppose, × ltd has a regular annual profit of Rs. 1,20,000 and the estimated capitalization is 10%. The capitalization in this case would be Rs.12,00,000. However, if the actual capitalization rate is 15% the capitalization would be 1,20,000/15 × 100 = Rs. 8,00,000

   The capitalization is higher by Rs.4,00,000 (12,00,000-8,00,000). It is the result of under-capitalization of the rate of capitalization.

Disadvantages of Over Capitalization

1. *Reduction in Dividend:* An over capitalized company earns a lower return. Hence, it is forced to reduce the dividend. It may even skip the dividend.
2. *Fall in market value:* The lower return on capital and cut in dividend adversely affect the market value of shares.
3. *Window Dressing:* In order to conceal the poor earnings, the company may resort to questionable accounting practices like inflating the value of stock, not providing for depreciation etc.
4. *Liquidation:* As over capitalized company may avoid even essential expenditure like maintenance of plant, due to the pressure on profits. It will further aggravate the problem.
5. *Waste of Resources:* An over capitalized company is unable to earn a decent return on its investment. Scarce resources are wasted because of inefficiency.
6. *Cut in wages:* An over capitalized company, may cut wages to improve profits. The workers will resent such action and industrial relations will be affected.

Remedies

An over capitalized company is often compared to a very fat person. He will suffer from various health problems. Unless serious efforts are taken at the earliest and the weight is reduced, his life will come to an untimely end. An over capitalized company must therefore take drastic steps for reorganization.

Reorganization is not easy. Depending on the intensity of the problem, it calls for sacrifice on the part of lenders and shareholders.

The following remedial measures are generally adopted.

1. Repayment of high cost dept
2. Reduction in interest rates through negotiations with the lenders
3. Reduction in the claims of lenders, debenture holders, financial institutions.

4. Reduction in the rate of preference dividend.
5. Reduction in the number of equity shares.
6. Reduction in the par value of equity shares

Under Capitalization

Under capitalization is the opposite of over capitalization. If the actual capitalization is less than standard capitalization, the company is said to be under capitalized.

Earnings of the company	Rs. 3 Crores
Rate of capitalization	Rs. 15%
Proper (or) standard capitalization	
3/15 × 100 = Rs. 20 crores	
Actual capitalization	Rs. 10 crores

The actual capitalization of the company is Rs. 10 Crores.

It is less than the standard capitalization of Rs. 20 crores. Hence, the company is under capitalized. In other words, for the earning, achieved by the company, the capitalization is low. The company earns a return of 30% which is considerably higher than the prevailing rate of return.

Disadvantages

1. *Attracts competition:* The earnings are significantly high, compared to the level of capitalization. The actual return in our example is an high as 30%. Such fabulous return attracts competitions.
2. *Demand for higher wages:* The earnings and dividends of the company are high. The workers are tempted to demand higher wages.
3. *Customer dissatisfaction:* The abnormally high rate of earnings attracts attention. The customers may feel that they are exploited by the company.
4. *Government control:* The Government may interfere and impose price restrictions or levy higher taxes.

Remedies

The situation of under capitalization may be corrected by the following steps.

1. *Issue of Bonus Shares:* Issue of bonus shares increases the number of shares and the amount of share capital. As a result, the earning per share or the rate of return on share capital is reduced. Dividend per share will also be less. The total earnings continue to be high. But the EPS and DPS after bonus issue appear to be low, as the earnings are spread on large number of shares.
2. *Splitting the shares*: This is also known as stock split. The face value of the share may be split leading to an increase in the number of shares. (For example a share of the face value of Rs.100 may be split into 10 shares of Rs. 10 each). There will be no change in the amount of share capital or the rate of earning. But the earning per share and dividend per share will decline to an apparently normal level.
3. Revaluation of assets: The book value of assets may be revised upwards. The share capital may also be increased correspondingly. The share holders may be given shares of higher face value in exchange for the shares held by them. This method has the effect of increasing capitalization to match the level of earnings.

Both over capitalization and under capitalization are bad. But over capitalization is a more serious problem. It is dangerous to the company, shareholders and the society. Drastic steps and sacrifice on the part of stakeholders are necessary to correct over capitalization.

Under capitalization on the other hand is not a serious problem. It is only a problem of adjustment of capital structure and can be easily corrected.